The American South

TOWNS &CITIES

Miller Park.
Chattanooga, Tennessee.

The American South

TOWNS & CITIES

WILLIAM A. BAKE / JAMES J. KILPATRICK

OXMOOR HOUSE, Inc. BIRMINGHAM

Library of Congress Catalog Number: 82-80593
ISBN: 0-8487-0533-5
Manufactured in the United States of America

First Printing

The American South: Towns & Cities

Editor-in-Chief John Logue
Editor Karen Phillips Irons
Production Manager Jerry Higdon
Associate Production Manager Joan Denman

FRONTISPIECE: *Timeless Dusk*.
Savannah, Georgia.

Contents

Southern Light.
Belhaven; Jackson, Mississippi.

Preface

Belhaven is one of those quiet older sections, though more modest than some. The streets are tree-shaded and seem wider than they are, probably because many people park their cars off-street. Most of us would be satisfied to live there with neighbors we have known for years, sharing, permitting, but perhaps not accepting, each others' weaknesses.

I pulled over to the curb in front of Eudora Welty's house about 6:15 p.m. The sun was still high in the summer sky, but the house was quiet. If she were home, how would she feel about a stranger stopping at suppertime? "Miss Welty," as they call her: recipient of the 1973 Pulitzer Prize for Fiction, member of the American Academy of Arts and Letters, author of dozens of short stories and five novels—a Southern treasure. I worried about making an unannounced visit, but I did want to say that I appreciated her work.

Jackson, Mississippi, was by no means the first Southern city in my current series of travels. I thought back to other cities and unplanned visits. In Baltimore, I stopped by a visitor information booth at Hopkins Plaza. Fresh into town and confused about locations, I asked the elderly lady behind the counter for directions to

Autumn at Invershiel.
Avery County, North Carolina.

ix

Charles Place. Perhaps she recognized the traveler's need for conversation in me for soon our conversation broadened, ranging to family and my work.

"Do you have a place to stay?" she eventually asked. "I'll have an extra room beginning Monday. It's a big house and the room is free."

"But you don't know me," I protested, obviously surprised.

"You have an honest face," she explained. The matter was settled in her mind.

In Savannah, a large white Victorian house caught my eye. Pyracantha spiraled around the porch pillars, its waxy red berries gleaming in the morning sun. From the porch, I could probably make a photograph of the berries, railing, and a row of houses across Habersham Street. "Certainly," the owner assented, responding to my knock on the front door and request.

"Walk anywhere on the porch. Take all the pictures you want."

A few minutes later I heard the door open. "When you're finished, come in," the owner called.

My host and his wife were in the parlor putting finishing touches on the most glorious Christmas tree I had ever seen. Reaching high to the nine-foot ceiling, it was literally covered with thousands of antique and collectible ornaments.

"We decorate it over a period of a week," they explained. "Everything is done by plan; too much is here to begin haphazardly." I examined tinsel from the 1800s, stars carved from ivory, and royal wedding ornaments from decades long faded from living memory. The tree was beautiful, but more than that, it contained an unwritten cultural history of events epic and small during the past century.

Shreveport, Little Rock, New Orleans, and Amarillo offered similar experiences. People to whom I was a complete stranger consistently invited me into their homes and shared their hospitality. Despite reports that our cities are dead-bolted and in decline, I could conclude only that Southerners—even in cities—retain an underlying trust and optimism. Such enduring traits, combined with a grand influx of economic power and youthful vigor, have created an urban renaissance in the South.

I do not mean that urban problems have melted away under the Southern sun. Two realities struggle for supremacy in the cities. Newfound economic power, boldly visible, is one. Glass-sheathed skyscrapers, restored landmark buildings, cascading fountains, and imposing sculptures proclaim its importance. The other reality, un-seen by many of us, is the struggle for livability. Declining tax bases, crime, and a massive influx of unskilled labor threaten even the gains made by economic boom. The ancient urban paradox still stalks us: Cities seem to stimulate the best and worst of human tendencies.

In the Garden District of New Orleans, power and problems endemic to poverty share the same space. The District is serene. Old homes grace tree-shaded streets there. It seems a fine place to live. But you also notice the small placards warning of security systems. Long iron fences encircle houses, and guard dogs watch from

Neighborhoods on the Gulf.
Galveston, Texas.

Sentries in Stone.
Alabama War Memorial; Montgomery, Alabama.

porches and driveways. Private patrol cars cruise the streets. This is wealth at bay. Crime—or the threat of it—threatens to keep increasing numbers of us behind locked doors.

I anticipated these problems, but found them to be less a priority than adjusting to the pace of the project. The task was to record my impressions—not to be journalistic; this would be a glimpse through artist's eyes. Fifty cities in seven months with three days for each of the largest and two—or one—for the others. I would do brief basic research and then rely on skill and circumstance. Sometimes from rental cars, but more often on foot, I explored downtowns, commercial districts, historic areas, and neighborhoods. From this perspective, I slowly developed my firsthand overview of urban life and attitude from Baltimore west to El Paso.

The unexpected was literally around the next corner. Carrying thirty-five pounds of expensive camera equipment, I felt vulnerable—and was. In one city, a young man approached me and stood watching me as I worked with a large tripod-mounted camera. "That's *nice*," he told me, avoiding eye contact. "How much you figure it's worth?" I lied, not very well, and kept working. Directly across the street, services were about to begin at a downtown church. Four ushers stood on the steps watching us, but soon everyone would be inside. I worked fast, finished, and walked off down the street. My visitor continued on his way in the opposite direction, but I knew he could double back very quickly. I glanced over my shoulder—

he was still walking away from me—and darted behind a building and through a parking lot. Reaching my car, I heaved my equipment in and locked the door. He was there as soon as I did it, running through the lot, looking, but not expecting me to be in a car so quickly. I pulled out and saw him standing halfway down the block, scanning the street.

The exception does not make the rule. These cities are not besieged fortresses. Pride and power permeate them. People everywhere are convinced their cities must be among the best of places. I saw it in the new downtowns, heard its echoes along the restored waterfronts, even felt it in the rumble of heavy industry. Stereotypes crumbled; I began to list cities I would like to live in. Not the obvious choices, but the surprises: Montgomery, Tulsa, Frankfort, Shreveport, Jackson, Greenville, Chattanooga, Richmond, and Lubbock—to name some. Unless you have reason to know them, you might never discover these eminently livable cities. In the South the verdict seems to have been rendered; we have somehow not only survived our past but have drawn upon the best of it to create a region reborn. Historians writing a century from now will remember these years as the best of times for cities in the South.

Eudora Welty was not home that evening. The sun filtered softly through the pines and a bluejay barked somewhere back in the yard, but there was nothing else. I stood for a moment in the driveway, disappointed, letting memories, many of them images, drift through my mind. Far to the east, sunlight would still be lingering along the Atlantic Coast. Across the Piedmont and mountains it might be drawing long shadows from the high-rise cities and small towns. I knew it must be burnishing the rivers and bayous of the Mississippi Valley with bronze and shining impassively down on the Plains and mountains to the west. In a sense all this—the entire South—is her home, just as it is mine. Mississippi is its microcosm; a thousand miles and three centuries of tradition are its reality.

A sentence Eudora Welty had written ten years earlier came back to me: "If the exposure is essential, still more so is the reflection."[1] She was referring to human experience and its effect on the inner person. As a photographer, I gave it special meaning. Exposing the film does not make the photograph; even more important is the interaction between artist and subject. "The sharpest recognition," she called it—that ultimate bonding of person and place.

Suddenly I felt satisfied. Her struggle for that recognition was verbal; mine was visual. Hers drew inspiration from the traditional South; mine encompassed the high-rise cities as well. But we were about the same thing: the experience of being both Southern and universally human. To that, these pages are dedicated.

Boone, North Carolina   William A. Bake
February 1982

1. Eudora Welty, *One Time, One Place* (New York: Random House, 1971), p. 8.

"Look Ahead—Look South."
Birmingham, Alabama.

The American South

TOWNS &CITIES

Of Southerners and Southern Cities

Half a century has passed since a band of twelve Southern writers delivered themselves of a manifesto. They called themselves the Nashville Agrarians, and they titled their work, *I'll Take My Stand.* Both individually and collectively, that is exactly what they did: They took a stand in 1931 in defense of a distinctively *Southern* way of life.

My purpose here is to have a look at the South of the Agrarians' day and, without getting too statistical about it, to have a look at the South today. More particularly, my thought is to visit a few favorite Southern cities and, without getting into the stuff of guidebooks, to reminisce about some of the men and women who have been identified with those cities. The Agrarians loved the country and feared the cities. I cherish an affection for both elements of the South—for the rural scenes that William Bake photographed so beautifully in *The American South: Four Seasons of the Land,* and for the city dwellers whose lives he has here recorded.

Who are we, we Southerners? Is there anything distinctive about our people and our region? By "the South," I mean to embrace the eleven states of the old Confederacy, plus Maryland, Kentucky and Oklahoma, but to speak in this context of *the*

South is to risk a confusion of terms at the outset. There is no such thing as *the* South. We are many Souths, ranging from Baltimore to Amarillo, from Louisville to Brownsville. The diversity of our land is more notable than its uniformity.

Even so, the fourteen States share a common inheritance. We are popularly lumped together for economic and social analysis. Historically and traditionally, the South has been as much a state of mind as a piece of real estate. My thesis is that there remains at least *a* definable South, that it retains certain distinctive elements, and that in some of our cities our region has something special to offer.

The twelve Agrarians had little use for the cities. Their principal concern was to ward off the factories and mills and smokestacks that in 1931 already were threatening the tranquillity of rural life. The fact of change could not be questioned, but was the change progress? The Agrarians thought not. The pursuit of happiness had turned into a "nervous running around which is without the logic, even, of a dog chasing its tail." They wanted none of the new technology. Southerners, they warned, should dread industrialism as they would dread "a pizen snake."

To the Agrarians, there was much more to life than mere getting and spending. They pleaded for rehabilitation of a rural economy and "the old individualism" associated with it. Underlying their manifesto was a passionate love of the land. They championed family and neighborhood and community. Their purpose was to preserve both the closeness and the isolation that all countrymen recognize. They saw their rural South as a South of small farms and large plantations, a paradise of rivers and bayous and coastal waters, a land of forests and woodlots and upland game. Small towns could be tolerated, even welcomed, but large cities were anathema. In this they stood with Thomas Jefferson. "I view great cities as pestilential to the morals, the health, and the liberties of man," said the Sage of Monticello. At least one of the Agrarians despised even the extension of macadam highways: The hard slick surface of such fancy roads, he complained, was hard on the feet of his mules. Paved highways could serve only to impose an alien materialism on a region "which prefers religion to science, handcraft to technology, the inertia of the fields to the acceleration of industry, and leisure to nervous prostration."

The twelve Southerners championed not only neighborhood and community, but something more besides. They spoke without embarrassment of what Thoreau called the "universal intelligence." To dwell close to nature is to comprehend the presence of a grand design—the slow turning of the seasons, the rhythmic cycles of planting, growth, harvest, and decay. It is also to stand in awe of the power of nature and to accept the commonplace miracles of everyday life on a farm. Whether we call this recognition metaphysics, or religion, or reverence for a supreme being, it forms the very foundation of lives that are lived close to the soil.

Implicitly or explicitly, the Agrarians of 1931 spoke in defense of other characteristics. They perceived the South of their day in terms of manners, civility, Edmund

Burke's "unbought grace of life." They liked the slower pace of a contemplative hour. Southerners, it was thought, had different ways of pursuing their leisure time, and they had more leisure time in which to pursue them. The Agrarians saw the South in terms of its history; the house of their fathers was shuttered in memories of recent defeat. Necessarily, as products of their generation, they acknowledged the pervasive presence of the Negro people, coexisting in the glass-chambered intimacy that was characteristic of the time.

The leading Agrarians were poets. Doubtless they tended to romanticize. Even as they hymned the glories of country living, the South was heading into a decade of dustbowls and economic miseries. Nothing good could be said of 10-cent cotton. For the nine million black residents, the hardships of poverty were compounded by the humiliations of segregation. Even then little remained of virgin forests and untilled land.

But when all this had been taken into account, it remains to be said that the Nashville Agrarians were right in their basic premises. The South was indeed a distinctive region, and it was in truth still wedded to rural life. The country as a whole had gone urban by 1920, but in 1930 only Florida and Maryland had shifted from a predominantly rural to a predominantly urban population. In Mississippi, Arkansas and the Carolinas, three of every four persons then lived in the country. As the Agrarians insisted, it was a generally good life, marked by small gratifications that were seen as large rewards. I was only eleven years old when *I'll Take My Stand* appeared—a small, skinned-knee product of Louisiana and Oklahoma—but I too would cheerfully have stood with the Nashville band.

What now? In 1981 another group of Southern essayists produced a semi-centennial volume, *Why the South Will Survive*. They invited Andrew Lytle, one of the original Nashville band, to contribute an afterword.

"Family and neighborhood made the world we inhabited," he wrote. "Travel through the countryside today and you will find it empty. People dwell there, but as individuals, except in certain stubborn and traditional pockets. They do not compose a community. Travel to the towns and small cities and they all look stamped out of plastic. They differ mainly in size. The outskirts hold flat buildings of assembly plants owned from afar; more sinisterly, factories dealing in chemical poisons pollute the countryside. People are beginning to have an anonymous look. . . .

"So the Agrarians failed. We failed at least to make any practical impact upon the amoeba-like growth of the machine and its technology. Only recently has it come to me why this is so. No man can know why, but I will venture this: None is prepared for the violent revolution which changes the nature of the familiar. I feel that this is why the communities threatened with extinction only sympathized with the book's protest. They could not believe that *their* way of living would disappear. Well, it has."

Most of us who live in the South and travel widely in the South probably would agree with much of Andrew Lytle's melancholy epilogue. Empirical evidence of change abounds. Only Mississippi and North Carolina are still predominantly rural—53 percent in the one case, 52 percent in the other. All the rest have joined in a march toward city life. Oklahoma and Virginia, once two-thirds rural, are two-thirds urban now. Farm populations have dropped by half in Georgia and Louisiana. Only one of five Texans now lives in the country.

And if it were not for the neat tabulations of the Bureau of the Census, the evidence of our own eyes and ears would confirm the homogenization of the South. We are as afflicted as other regions with architectural rick-rack and ticky-tack, with six-pack suburbs and miles of store-bought chicken. A region that would not bow to old King George now genuflects to monarchs of another day, King Burger and King Wiener. The freeways of Atlanta are as clogged as the freeways of Cleveland. We traffic as others do, in jams.

Fifty years ago the South was a land of truly distinctive speech, of twang and drawl and dropped "r's." Here and there these accents persist; the young ladies of Richmond, encountering one another at Miller & Rhoads, still cry the old greeting: "Hah theah! Har're yew?" But year by year the accents fade. As recently as 1945, in Virginia's Northern Neck, you could hear the dipthongs toppling; the ma-oose still ran ab-oot the ha-oose. In Charleston, to mail a photograph you needed a piece of cyuorrogated cyardbode. In Arkansas, the housewife who abandoned Piggly-Wiggly would go to the A-ya & P-ya instead.

If this housewife lived in Forrest City or Jonesboro, she might drive to Mimphis, Tinnessee, to shop. Southern speech was a generous speech; it gave you long pauses and slow cadences, and generally two syllables for one, or five for three. Nowadays most Southerners talk as if they'd been raised in Omaha or Salt Lake City.

And yet, and yet . . . a convincing case can be made that the South remains a markedly distinctive region of the country. In little ways and large ways, in good ways and bad ways, we still identify ourselves as of the South, *Southern*. The old order changes, but it may not have changed as greatly as we often believe. And a Southland that once was distinguished by the quality of its rural life now may claim a certain something—an ambience, if you please—that sets some of its cities apart from the general sprawl.

Who are we? And what makes several Southern cities exceptional?

In 1931, there were about 36 million of us. As this is written in mid-1982, we have a little more than doubled. Fifty years ago only two of our fourteen States were predominantly urban. Today only two are still predominantly rural.

The ethnic mix has changed dramatically, most notably in the central cities. Washington, D.C., reported a black population of 70 percent in 1980 and Atlanta a black component of almost 67 percent. Black residents outnumber white residents in Richmond, New Orleans, Baltimore, Birmingham and in dozens of smaller towns and cities also. Owing largely to the Voting Rights Act of 1965, these ethnic changes have brought political changes with them. Virtually no Negro citizens held public office in 1930. By 1980, at least 2,000 black officeholders could be counted. In the one-party South of the Agrarians' day, the Negro vote scarcely mattered; today the black vote is often decisive.

As rural population has declined, our cities have grown enormously. We have gone from silos to skyscrapers. Between 1930 and 1980, Miami's metropolitan population ballooned from 132,000 to 1,600,000 and Atlanta's from 371,000 to more than two million. Houston approaches three million residents and at 5 o'clock on any weekday afternoon, so they say, cars outnumber people three to one.

Out in the countryside, small farms have yielded to large farms, and large farms and ranches have yielded to agri-business conglomerates. In Texas they count the cattle from Piper Cubs. Some Texans do, anyhow. Fifty years ago our economy depended largely on tobacco, cotton, peanuts and livestock. These still are important— the Cotton Exchange in Memphis still does a lively trade—but Southern agriculture has diversified into fruits, vegetables, soybeans and pulpwood. Meanwhile, the factories, mills and refineries so feared by the Agrarians have raised their smokestacks everywhere.

Behind some of the phenomenal figures on growth is the recent phenomenon known to demographers as "in-migration." Over a span of 80 years, from Reconstruction to the mid-fifties, the South lost population. Then the outgoing tide began to turn. Native-born Southerners decided to stay put. The black exodus slowed and halted. To the great enrichment of Southern communities, relocated industries brought the importation of relocated managers. Our work force changed as more women and more minorities entered growing job markets. The whole economy has moved in directions the Agrarians would have disapproved.

The South was the poorest region in 1930, in terms of material wealth, and it still is the poorest. As recently as 1959, more than 35 percent of all Southern families were below the poverty level. That figure has been cut in half. The gap steadily closes between workers in the Southern States and workers elsewhere; and besides, we cling serenely to the notion that material wealth isn't the be-all and end-all anyhow.

Rising levels of education have contributed significantly to the social and economic changes. The most dramatic changes, of course, have resulted from the Supreme Court's desegregation decision in 1954. Back in 1930 our public schools were separate but God knows they weren't equal. In that year Alabama, Florida, Georgia and Mississippi were spending five times as much on the education of every white child as they were spending on every black child. Over much of the South, black youngsters of high school age weren't in school: No high schools were provided for them. The old inequalities in public education have been eliminated almost everywhere in the South. With few exceptions, desegregation has come more smoothly to the South, with less violence and animosity, than in other regions—and this, I believe, the Agrarians might well have foreseen.

The pervasive influence of our Southern churches—chiefly Protestant churches—has contributed to the acceptance of social change. This is not to suggest that our churches have fully integrated, for few of them have, but the Christian ethic is strongly felt. The South remains the most "religious" of all regions, at least in terms of professed active church membership. In the Deep South, 96 percent of all families reportedly are identified with one church or another, and 83 percent name a Protestant denomination. The voice of the radio preacher is abroad in our land. Georgia has more than 20 stations that broadcast nothing but religious messages and music from early morning until late at night. I can't prove it, but I'm certain the South has proportionately more Sunday schools, Bible classes, gospel singers, church suppers and revivals than other regions. Supreme Court or no Supreme Court, hundreds of rural schools still have prayers in their classrooms.

If the role of religion has remained constant, the political picture has changed remarkably. In the 80 years that followed Appomattox and Reconstruction, the South exhibited a political pattern for which it became famous. Ours was the one-party Democratic South. There were occasional falls from grace. Tennessee went for Harding in 1920, and Kentucky liked McKinley in 1896 and Coolidge in 1924, but except for the upheaval of 1928, the solid South stayed solid. Some of the Democratic majorities were downright impressive. Roosevelt carried South Carolina in 1932 by a margin of 44 to 1. Republicans were rare birds. When the Agrarians took their stand in 1931, the South had no Republicans in the U.S. Senate and only seven Republicans in the House.

Commencing in 1948, that pattern fell apart. Four Southern States rumped off for States Righter J. Strom Thurmond. In 1956 seven went for Eisenhower. In 1964 five went for Goldwater. In 1968 only Texas stayed in the Democratic corral, and in 1972 they all jumped the fence. They all came home to the Democrats with Carter in 1976, and then they all—all but Georgia—went off again with Reagan in 1980. At local levels and in the State legislatures, Republicans have made relatively few inroads, but in its national politics the one-party South has gone the way of the one-hoss shay.

In the Agrarians' day, a Confederate tradition still was widely revered. Hundreds of faded veterans of the Lost Cause were still alive, thin gray men in their late 80s and 90s. On Confederate Memorial Day the South's battle flag flew everywhere.

8

The United Daughters of the Confederacy then numbered 60,000 members. Little of the old spirit remains. The Daughters are down to 26,000 now, and the battle flags fly mainly at roadside stands that sell souvenirs and cider. In Hattiesburg, Mississippi, a stony Confederate soldier stands in the courthouse square, eternally fixed at parade rest, but a TV tower looks over his shoulder. We still hear rebel yells when a band plays "Dixie," and some of the old regimental flags still are glass-cased in the Georgia capital, but things have changed—and changed for the better. Not far from those Georgia flags hangs a portrait of Martin Luther King, Jr., and up in Columbia the Sons of Secession at Fort Sumter have honored Mary McLeod Bethune.

One other major change in the South merits a word. H. L. Mencken's scathing essay, "The Sahara of the Bozart," appeared in his second volume of *Prejudices* in 1920. My generation grew up in glum agreement with the essential accuracy of Mencken's indictment. Down in Dixie, he had charged, "a poet is now almost as rare as an oboe-player, a dry-point etcher or a metaphysician." In all that gargantuan paradise of the fourth-rate, "there is not a single picture gallery worth going into, or a single orchestra capable of playing the nine symphonies of Beethoven, or a single opera house, or a single theater devoted to decent plays, or a single public monument worth looking at, or a single workshop devoted to making beautiful things."

Mencken at this point had barely warmed up: "When you come to critics, musical composers, painters, sculptors, architects and the like, you will have to give it up, for there is not even a bad one between the Potomac mudflats and the Gulf. Nor a historian. Nor a philosopher. Nor a theologian. Nor a scientist. In all these fields the South is an awe-inspiring blank—a brother to Portugal, Serbia and Albania."

There was more to Mencken's essay—painfully much more—but it was impossible not to acknowledge a core of truth in his apple of extravagance. The war of 1861-65 had in fact drained the South of her finest leadership and her main sources of material wealth. In the hard struggle merely to survive, the South found little time left for preserving the nine symphonies of Beethoven. The Agrarians of 1931 were more concerned with preserving the feet of mules.

The sixty-odd years since Mencken's essay have been years of phenomenal regeneration. Thirty-two major orchestras (those with annual operating income in excess of $2.5 million) are nationally in operation. Seven of them are in the South. Of 36 regional orchestras listed by the American Symphony League, thirteen are in the South. Smaller metropolitan orchestras are all over the place, along with opera companies, dance companies, choral groups and theater companies. The museums of fine art in Houston, Dallas, Richmond and other cities may be no match for the museums of New York, Philadelphia and Chicago, but they house excellent collections nonetheless. In 1930 the South had 31 percent of the nation's population but

Colossus and the Lady.
Baltimore & Ohio Railroad Museum; Baltimore, Maryland.

11

only 11 percent of all book sales. By 1972, still at 31 percent total population, the South had 23 percent of book sales and 28 percent of all bookstores.

I don't mean to overdo it. A 1980 analysis of radio programming found only one classical station in Arkansas and only two such stations in the whole of Georgia. The South's radio waves vibrate overwhelmingly to the strains of country, Western, and rock—that is, when they are not vibrating to the fulminations of the radio clergy. We provide by far the largest market for the sale of banjos, mandolins, and flat-top guitars. Economically speaking, the grass may be greener somewhere else, but the grass is bluer in Dixie. We buy fewer classical recordings than are sold in other areas, but sales of gospel records are ten times higher in the South than in the second-ranking region. We are not much on *Harper's, Atlantic,* or *National Review,* but we buy 30 percent of *Penthouse,* 34 percent of all comic books, and more than half the copies of *American Field.* Of learned societies we have very few; of Rotarians, Kiwanians, Optimists and Elks we have whole battalions. The Wrigley's gum people ran a survey in mid-January 1982. In the preceding week, 60 percent of all Southerners had chewed at least one stick of gum. No other region could make that claim.

So, who are we?

We are Southerners. Within our own region, we have changed considerably since the Agrarians were writing in 1931. We are more citified, more hispanic, proportionally less black. Our schools have changed; our politics have changed; our adherence to certain customs and traditions has changed. In some ways, we have hardly changed at all. Our women still marry younger, have more children, and hold fewer jobs in private employment than the women of other regions. We are still poor in material wealth, though gaps are closing. We still have more illiteracy than other regions have. We still are gun-slingers and gospel-singers, and we still evince an intensity of regional pride that is unmatched anywhere else. This is our South, and we love it.

Unlike the Agrarians of fifty years ago, we cherish our cities. It bears repeating, in the name of simple candor, that not all our cities are distinctive. In the whole of the country, probably not more than a score of major cities could be so defined. Throughout the length and breadth of the Republic, when you've seen one supermarket or shopping mall, you've seen 'em all. Our traffic lights flash red, green and amber, just like everyone else's; our skyscrapers are just as glassy, just as boxy, as the skyscrapers of Seattle and Detroit. Same hotels and motels. Same french-fries. Yet a traveler who meanders from Baltimore to El Paso—especially a traveler with Bill Bake's camera eye—finds the experience richly rewarding. And if we travel back and forth in time, as Southerners are wont to do, past and present commingle as gently as this year's annuals in the past century's gardens.

Begin with Baltimore. No city in the land, not even San Francisco, has done a more exciting job of restoring a neglected waterfront than Baltimore has done. As recently as 1970, the area was a rat-ridden slum. Now it bustles with life and color. Move on to Annapolis. Is there a more charming state capital? I cannot recall one. Drive on to Washington. By its very nature, the District of Columbia has to be distinctive, but in recent years the city has gained a quality of life it never had before. Washington in springtime is the loveliest capital in the world.

Jacob and Annita Fountains.
Hopkins Plaza; Baltimore, Maryland.

13

FOR FIRE
BREAK GLASS
OPEN DOOR
PULL HANDLE
DOWN ONCE
LET GO

156

FIRE

Silent Bandstand.
U.S. Naval Academy; Annapolis, Maryland.

The Constellation at Nightfall.
The Inner Harbor; Baltimore, Maryland.

Row Houses on N. Linwood.
Baltimore, Maryland.

Oddfellows.
Fells Point; Baltimore, Maryland.

Harborplace Reflections.
Baltimore, Maryland.

City Traffic.
N. Charles & W. Fayette Streets;
Baltimore, Maryland.

16

Business as Tradition.
Lexington Market; Baltimore, Maryland.

and Sons
OUR SPECIALITY
FANCY FRUIT BASKETS
MADE TO ORDER FOR ALL
OCCASSIONS F&G 15-16
THYME
PARSLEY
ONIONS
Tropicana
Orange Juice
Grapefruit
Juice
Cantaloupe
Honey Dew
HORSERADISH
SOLD HERE
LIMES
we accept
FRESH GRATED HOT
FANCY
FRUITS AND PRODUCE
HAM
PORK
POULTRY
79
49
69
98

Neighbors on Hanover Street.
Richmond, Virginia.

Richmond Stayed Staid

I would lead you into Virginia by way of Alexandria's Old Town, and pause in unspoiled Fredericksburg, and take a side trip to born-again Williamsburg, for these are cameos to treasure. The immediate destination is Richmond, where William Byrd in 1633 laid out a city by the noble James, where Patrick Henry lit a torch of liberty, where a doomed Confederacy had its capital.

You will understand that I write of Richmond with a special affection. There I came in the spring of 1941, a scared cub, to take my first job in newspapering. There I met, wooed and wed my wife. There I remained for 25 happy years. The city changes. It has lost some of the gentler elements—the patina on bronze—that once softened the hard inheritance of Reconstruction days. Even so, the essential aspects of Richmond are still there. Richmond survives like one of the great estates of England: The city's soul is the soul of gentry, but a ticket-taker stands at the gate.

Let me remember. It was March 1941, and I had completed the baccalaureate requirements of Columbia's *Universitatis Missouriensis.* That is how the parchment read. The wide world crooked an insistent finger. Because I am a day person, I wanted to work on an afternoon paper; because I am by instinct and inheritance a

Southerner, I wanted to work in the South. Letters of application went forth to Atlanta, to New Orleans, to Richmond—and behold there came back a telegram from Charles Henry Hamilton, then city editor of the Richmond *News Leader:* "Would you be interested in job as reporter starting $35 a week?" My reply reflected the brevity so beloved of my journalism professors: "Will report Monday."

The C&O train that bore me toward Virginia paused in Louisville long enough for reunion with a lovely lady, then chuffed slowly across a flooded Southland to let me off at Richmond's old Main Street Station. I spent the night in the Railway YMCA, and on Sunday morning walked through the Capitol grounds and up Franklin Street to Fourth. The building that then housed Richmond newspapers was not so posh as the building that houses the papers today, but it was Taj Mahal to a 20-year-old with ten dollars in his pocket and a sheepskin in his suitcase.

No one was home at the paper. Not even a guard answered my diffident knock. People didn't worry with security guards in those days. But in a side alley, where the newspaper trucks came to load their cargoes by the pressroom, an intoxicating smell still lingered from the night's pressrun—the smell of printer's ink. Since that day a benevolent providence has acquainted me with other enchanting aromas—the bouquet of fine Burgundies, the fragrance of beautiful women, the haunting smoke of hickory and applewood—but nothing is cleaner or sharper or more exhilarating than the smell of printer's ink. That is, if you like the stuff.

On Monday morning, freshly scrubbed and dressed in my best three-piece brown herringbone tweed with the double-breasted vest, I presented myself to Charlie Hamilton—130 pounds of breathless fledgling (breathless because it was a long walk from the Railway YMCA to Fourth Street)—and settled into a tobacco-burned desk with a two-piece telephone and an Underwood that had seen better days. Fifteen years after I had pronounced to an indifferent world a five-year-old's determination to become a newspaperman, I drew a delirious breath. The phone rang. "Rewrite," I said. "Kilpatrick."

Only six months before I came to town, the morning *Times-Dispatch* had been merged with the afternoon *News Leader* under the control of the Bryan family. Joseph Bryan, late in the 1800s, was the first of the newspaper clan. He was succeeded in 1908 by his son John Stewart, who was in turn succeeded in 1944 by his son Tennant, who was in turn succeeded in 1978 by his son Stewart. When I arrived on the scene, John Stewart was in charge. Almost daily he would come drifting through the city room, talking with reporters and editors, a six-footer as slender as a pole bean. Toward the end of his days he was white-tufted on top like a quizzical cockatoo, a quintessential gentleman who was friendly and reserved, kindly and authoritative, all in a breath.

I think of "Virginian," and John Stewart Bryan comes to mind. I think of "South Carolinian," and John Dana Wise comes to mind. He was general manager of the

Richmond newspapers. He had a face off a Roman coin, blue-chip eyes, silver hair, the most flawlessly tailored man I ever knew. Even in hunting gear, he seemed always to have stepped from the pages of a two-dollar magazine, immaculate, confident, exuding executive power. Deferential to women, courteous to men, Jack Wise was all fire and ice. He was largely self-educated, but he had read deeply in political philosophy and he held passionately to his conservative convictions. Somewhere along the line he introduced me to Edmund Burke's *Reflections on the Revolution in France.* He introduced me to John Randolph of Roanoke: "I am an aristocrat! I hate equality, I love liberty!" Jack Wise had despised Franklin Roosevelt; he held Truman in contempt; Eisenhower seemed no improvement. Under Kennedy the nation was drifting from all the old solid moorings. An egalitarian society and a welfare state were no part of a world he wanted to live in. So one morning in November 1963, dressed for the field, favorite shotgun in hand, he stopped that world and got off.

The most colorful character at the newspapers was Douglas Southall Freeman, the historian and editor. I have met orderly people in my time; I have known men of efficiency and discipline; I have encountered writers with tremendous productive capacity. But in these areas I have never known the equal of Douglas Southall Freeman. He was known as Dr. Freeman to his face and as "the Doc" behind his back. Born in 1886, he won his Ph.D degree in economics at an early age, developed a reputation as a tax specialist, and then turned to military history and to editorial writing. He became editor of the *News Leader* in 1915.

He was only in his mid-fifties when I met him in 1941, but he seemed much older. There was a certain venerable air about him. He had the tidy bay window of a prosperous archbishop, a large nose, a forehead splendidly domed. I remember black alpaca suits, starched shirts, wire-rimmed spectacles. He liked things small and neat and tidy; he typed on an elite typewriter and he wrote a nine-point longhand, each letter swiftly and separately formed. In his youth he had chewed tobacco, a habit he abandoned to cigarettes. Then he discovered to his consternation how much time he was wasting in lighting, puffing, and putting out. "Time alone is irreplaceable," read a misspelled motto over his wall clock. "Waste it not." He totted up the seconds and minutes that he was squandering to smoking every day. Then he threw away a half-consumed pack of cigarettes and never touched the weed again.

The Doc kept a schedule that became legendary in Richmond. He would arise at 3 o'clock from his monastic third-floor study, pack a parsimonious lunchpail, and drive downtown to the newspaper by way of Monument Avenue. As he went by the statue of Stonewall Jackson, he would nod. As he passed the monument to Jefferson Davis, again he would make a gesture of respect. But when he circled the monument to Lee, he would raise his hand in full salute. Anyhow that was the story we were told, and the Doc never troubled to deny it.

Arriving at his office at 3:30 or 4 o'clock he would plunge immediately into his day as editor of the *News Leader*. In the ensuing three hours he would write two thousand words of editorial copy. Now and then a reporter might contribute an editorial, but such occasions were rare. Six days a week, for all practical purposes, he wrote the whole works. He also edited the letters to the editor. He had his editorials set in solid ten-on-ten, 14 picas wide, and because he hated to waste space on headlines his page came out a dull Confederate gray.

Dr. Freeman's role was to be mentor to his city, to his State, to his nation, and to the erring nations of the world. So far as I can recall, he had not a spritely bone in his body. A man of ponderous dignity, he tended to write ponderous copy, the Gibbonesque sentences rolling magisterially through paragraphs of interminable length. Yet he could write with great force also, in tones of bell-like authority, and he commanded a formidable influence in public affairs.

The Doc's mornings thus were passed in editorial labors. He had two daily radio broadcasts, one at eight, the other at noon. His speaking pitch was somewhere around a sepulchural low C. After his final broadcast, he would pick up his lunch-pail and drive home for lunch. His custom was to take a brief nap. Then he began his second day as Douglas Southall Freeman, historian. For three hours he would labor over the crates of volumes and archives that were forever being trucked to his home. An hour was set aside for dinner, at which his children and his gracious but long-suffering wife could speak with him. Then it was back to his study until 10 o'clock, and thence to bed. On Sunday mornings he had a half-hour's broadcast from his home, "Lessons in Living," devoted to Baptist remonstrances. The program attracted a tremendous following.

In the mid-twenties, when he began research on his monumental *R. E. Lee*, the Doc began an exercise in vanity that he continued to his death. He would record every hour and minute spent on his books. In *Lee* he invested 6,100 hours, in *Lee's Lieutenants* 7,121 hours, and in his final work, *George Washington*, 15,693 hours. He worked from 5 x 7 notecards, color-coded for cross reference, and when he finally assembled all the cards required for a particular chapter, he typed at remarkable speed.

Toward the end of 1948, after 33 years of this regimen, Dr. Freeman abruptly wearied of the newspaper game. He summoned me to his paneled fourth-floor office and had me installed with the lofty title of associate editor. After six months under his tutelage, I was regarded as ready. Editorial writing, he told me, is "writing on sand," but if I wanted to succeed him as editor, good luck and God bless. If I ever needed his advice, I had only to telephone, but he would never look over my shoulder. He packed up his lunchpail, jammed his gray fedora on that massive head, and went home. Except for quarterly meetings of the newspaper's board, he never set foot in the *News Leader* again.

The Rotunda at Twilight.
University of Virginia; Charlottesville, Virginia.

I called him fairly often over the next few years, usually for counsel on local obituaries. Our paper had developed a considerable reputation for the high style in which we sent Virginians off to glory, and the Doc never let me down. There would be a brief, avuncular rumbling of the throat, and then he would dictate an editorial encomium perfectly suited to the occasion. The tributes sometimes got a little flowery, but his rule was to speak no evil of the dead. Once I had the temerity to suggest that he was spreading it on a little thick. Over the telephone I could sense a cheerful grin. "That will be apparent," he said, "to everyone who knew the old coot." And besides, he added, quoting Dr. Samuel Johnson, "in lapidary inscriptions a man is not upon his oath." I had the editorial set in type and without comment took a galley proof to Tennant Bryan. He read it and twinkled. "My, my," he said, "that sounds just like Dr. Freeman."

Once he left the paper, the Doc followed substantially his old schedule at home, piling up the minutes and hours on *Washington*. In May of 1953, at the luncheon he gave annually for Southern Railway directors, I asked him how the work was going. He was characteristically precise. Barring interruptions, he would finish Volume VI at 3:30 on the afternoon of Saturday, June 13. He was right on target. He finished Volume VI at 3:30 that afternoon, and that evening dropped dead of a heart attack.

Dr. Freeman was in a class by himself, but the Richmond of my early newspaper days had other colorful characters. After a few months on the rewrite desk, I was cut loose to cover the Main Street beat, then police and fire, then municipal courts, and in time the General Assembly, Supreme Court of Appeals, and the Governor's office. These were heady years for a young man in love with newspapering. Every profession, I suppose, has its moments of great exhilaration, but I would argue the proposition that nothing surpasses the best moments of a reporter's life. To go out on a breaking story, armed with nothing more than a copy pencil and a notebook; to cover that story competently; to write against a deadline; and an hour later to read your own smudgy creation, still warm from the press—this is the power and the glory. Did I say that nothing surpasses such a moment? Nothing even comes close.

My professors of journalism, sad to say, had left me almost wholly untutored in the law. I embarked upon court coverage as innocently ignorant as if I had just arrived from the Gobi, but Richmond was then blessed with an uncommonly able bench and bar. The Fourth U. S. Circuit was especially strong: Judge Armistead Dobie, who looked like Athos in *The Three Musketeers*; Judge John J. Parker, who looked like everybody's grandpa; and Judge Morris A. Soper, who looked like everybody's aunt. In one of the worst hours of its kind in the history of the United States Senate—an hour to be repeated years later with the nomination of Clement Haynsworth—the Senate had rejected Parker's nomination to the Supreme Court. We cannot know what bitterness he held in his heart, but I cannot recall a kinder figure on the bench. He welcomed a bewildered cub into his chambers, explained key points in the court's opinions, and loaned this youngster some of his own textbooks in pleading, practice, and constitutional law. Israel Steingold, a lawyer with a wide federal practice, became my late afternoon professor. In a matter of months I was soon rattling through the Richmond courts as glibly as any second-year student in a school of law.

In those days Richmond retained the old nomenclature for its tribunals. We had a Chancery Court, a Law and Equity Court, and a couple of Hustings Courts with both civil and criminal jurisdiction. We also had the lower courts, which operated straight from the ferocious pages of Dickens. By the time I arrived, the most notorious of our police court judges, John J. Crutchfield, had departed, but he had been succeeded by a spider-legged fellow, sallow-faced, whose twisted lips could curl unbelievably at the predominantly Negro defendants who came before him. The court then operated in the basement of City Hall, in a long room redolent of stale smoke and the stench of pervasive misfortune. The day's defendants were brought to court early in the morning and lodged in two cages at the rear of the room, one for whites, one for blacks. As each defendant's name was called, the miscreant walked a long gauntlet to the bench, there to face the fearful visage of the judge. Proceedings were swift, summary, and usually *in terrorem.*

Eventually all that changed. Police Court moved across Broad Street to what was known as "the annex" and there acquired at least some elements of decorum. Some of the old color remained: The regular Police Court lawyers continued to maintain their offices under the scraggly plane trees outside. Mr. Harris, by virtue of seniority, had the first tree; Mr. Gianniny had the second tree; and one of the city's most voluble lawyers, Mr. Carwile, had the third tree from the corner. Mr. Carwile's passionate pleas to the police justice were seldom successful, chiefly because his clients were almost invariably guilty as charged, but they were memorable forensic efforts.

At a higher level of jurisprudence, the Richmond courts offered other spectacular clashes. The city had streetcars in those days, and the streetcars occasionally ran down pedestrians. Such regrettable incidents produced suits against the power company, George E. Allen for the plaintiff and Archibald Robertson for the defendant. Allen was fox-sly, Robertson bull-stubborn. Allen was one of the first plaintiff's lawyers in the land to haul an articulated skeleton into a courtroom, the better to explain to a mesmerized jury just where the streetcar had crippled his client.

In the Richmond of my apprenticeship, criminal cases were mostly routine, but now and then a trial would come along, at once juicy and lucrative, and that meant Leith Bremner for the defense. He was short and stout, with a florid face as fat as a full moon. I'm not sure he truly suffered from chronic nasal congestion, but he had a way of wheezing in court whenever the prosecution seemed to be scoring a point.

Misty Summer Morning.
Colonial Williamsburg, Virginia.

Old City Hall to the James.
Richmond, Virginia.

Geraniums at the Window.
Alexandria, Virginia.

28

At especially critical moments, when an adverse witness had the jury's attention, Bremner would produce a handkerchief half the size of a tablecloth and, with an apologetic roll of his rheumy eyes, proceed to blow the jury's attention away.

My first Virginia Governor—the first one I covered regularly—was Colgate W. Darden, Jr., the finest man I ever met in public life. My second Governor, William M. Tuck, was the most colorful politician I ever encountered—and I have encountered some lulus. It was said in the pressroom that the "M." stood for Mountainous. Bill Tuck had the brobdingnagian build of a barrel of bourbon, perhaps because he had consumed such copious quantities of it. After the urbane Darden, many Virginians groaned at the prospect of a cigar-smoking, tobacco-spitting country lawyer from Halifax County, but Tuck surprised everyone. He made a superlative Governor. He won enactment of a tough water pollution law; he instituted a system of medical examiners to replace the old village coroners; he revitalized the state's antiquated mental hospitals; and when employees of the Virginia Electric & Power Company threatened to strike, he threatened in turn to invoke a colonial law empowering a Governor to muster every able-bodied male into the militia. He meant it, too. A fellow named Carey was then head of the International Brotherhood of Electrical Workers, a slender, dark-haired union activist. In his career with the IBEW, Carey had encountered every known form of intimidation by management, but he had never encountered a threat to turn his union members into militiamen with orders to stay on the job. I asked Carey what he thought of Tuck. "Cuh-razy," he mumbled. But he settled the dispute.

After his term as Governor, Tuck served in the House of Representatives from Virginia's Fifth District. In 1952 we traveled together to the Democratic National Convention in Chicago. That was the convention that almost expelled Southern Democrats from the party. On the night of a crucial vote, I rode to the stockyards in a taxi with my ebullient friend. He had put away a 20-ounce steak and a fifth of Jim Beam, and he was r'aring for action. He regaled the driver and me with the greatest farewell address since Lee said goodbye to his troops. "If you must drive us from the house of our fathers," he cried, "then we will go into the darkness with our hearts broken but with our principles unshaken." Here his wattles quivered and his eyes misted. The cab driver kept glancing back uneasily as the orator expounded the sound doctrine of States' rights. It was some speech, but alas, only the driver and I ever heard it. At the crucial moment on the floor of the convention, Big Bill struggled toward his feet to seek recognition from the chair. John Daffron of the Associated Press and I somehow entangled our feet with his. Meanwhile, Virginia's Governor John S. Battle, head of the delegation, was on his way to the lectern. Tuck sat balefully in his place while Battle saved the day for Southern Democrats.

In the years of this reminiscence, Richmond had no notable restaurants but it had two great oyster bars, one at Murphy's Hotel, the other at Rueger's. You could

The Doorman.
Hotel Roanoke; Roanoke, Virginia.

Wedding at Maymont.
Richmond, Virginia.

A Solid Clientele.
Roanoke, Virginia.

The Frost Diner.
Warrenton, Virginia.

get a dozen Chincoteagues for 35 cents and a great schooner of beer for a quarter. The city boasted two headwaiters of remarkable renown—Booker at the Hotel John Marshall, and Rush at the Commonwealth Club. Rush invented a dish compounded of thin corncakes, Smithfield ham and oysters; it has never been surpassed in the chronicles of Southern cooking. On special occasions, Rush himself would make mint juleps, signing each one in the silver's frost.

Richmond was a city of memorable great ladies. Fifty years ago several of them maintained apartments on the second floor of the Jefferson Hotel, with high-ceilinged rooms and French doors that opened above Franklin Street. The story is told of a young reporter, newly arrived in town, who was assigned to interview one of the grande dames. This was about 1941. She received the journalist with characteristic grace and charm, welcomed him to Richmond, and gently instructed him in the ways in which Virginians differed from other folk. "The first thing you must understand," she said, "is that we have lived longer under the flag of Great Britain than under the flag of the United States." I checked it out, subtracting 1607 from 1776 and 1776 from 1941, and by George, she was right.

Several other ladies contributed largely to the mystique of Richmond. One day in 1943, our obituary editor, Robert Beverley Munford, arranged for me to have tea with Ellen Glasgow. She was then nearly 70, but she still possessed those qualities of irony and wit that marked her novels. I don't suppose Richmonders have tea any more, but I remember the winter lamplight, antimacassars on Victorian chairs, a genteel clutter of books and cups, and photographs in silver frames. Richmond never knew quite what to make of Miss Glasgow. She and her friend James Branch Cabell were literary celebrities—they were oases in Mencken's "Sahara of the Bozart"—and as such the city was happy to claim them. But they were, well, you know, a little daring. Richmond is never daring. Richmond was staid then, and it has stayed staid.

Daisy Avery was cast in a different mold. She was for years a mainstay of the United Daughters of the Confederacy. Reporters knew her as Confederate Daisy, a redoubtable figure, full-rigged, white-haired, blue-eyed, often dismayed by the disappearance of the old gentility, but unyielding in her defense of the Southern way.

I dwell upon Richmond at such length not only because I lived there so long, and loved the city so dearly, but also because Richmond continues to symbolize so much that is distinctive about the older Southern cities. It is a city of reflections—reflections in the river, reflections in silver, reflections of family in the letterheads of the old law firms. When the wind is right, the faint fragrance of curing tobacco seeps up from the silent warehouses, and for Richmonders in exile the smell of tobacco holds the power of Eliot's spring rain, mixing memory and desire. They were twenty-five good years.

Range Cattle on Wilburn Ridge.
Grayson Highlands, Virginia.

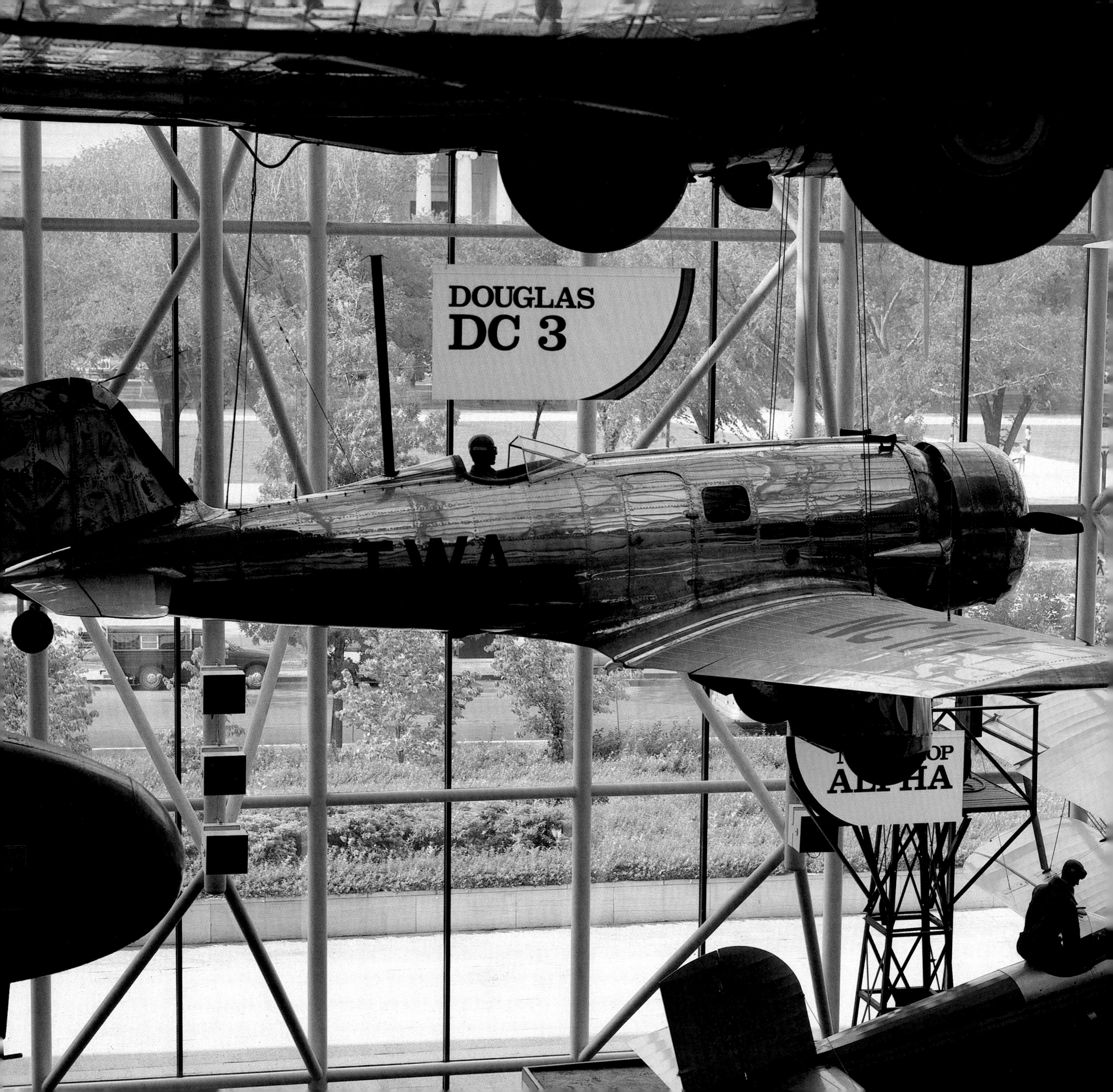
DOUGLAS
DC 3
TWA
ALPHA

Quiet Moment at the Capitol.
Washington, D.C.

Row Houses—District Style.
Bryant Street, N.W.; Washington, D.C.

Regatta at Cherry Blossom Time.
The Tidal Basin; Washington, D.C.

The Chosen of the Skies.
National Air and Space Museum; Washington, D.C.

Snow in the Shadows.
Old Salem; Winston-Salem, North Carolina.

Tarheel Horse Sense

T he towns of southern Virginia are not exactly hotbeds of excitement, except when the tobacco auctions are underway, and you won't find a great urban complex in the whole of North Carolina. There are such attractive coastal towns as Manteo and Nag's Head and Wilmington, such nice mountain towns as Asheville and Boone, and there are fine mill towns and furniture towns, but Charlotte is the only city of more than 300,000 population in the state and only four other cities have more than 100,000. Winston-Salem is notable for its activities in the arts, and Chapel Hill and Durham for their great universities, but that's about the size of it.

I have a special memory of Durham. I came to the Richmond *News Leader* in March of 1941. On a Sunday morning eight months later, my deskmate and I decided to have a look at Duke University. An old friend from my college days, Mary Eidam, was teaching cello in Duke's conservatory and playing in the university orchestra. Stan and I went around to the great Gothic chapel where Handel's *Messiah* was being performed and spent an hour listening to that magnificent hymn to peace on earth. We emerged into the winter twilight a little before 5 o'clock, carrying Mary's cello, and walked across the campus talking of music and old friends. A

newsboy came running toward us crying "Extra!" He was peddling the Durham *Herald,* and it was Pearl Harbor.

In any roll call of distinguished universities in our land, Duke at Durham and the University of North Carolina at Chapel Hill would rank well up in the ranks— not only for basketball but for academics as well. UNC has a venerable history. It opened its doors in January 1795, and for the first two weeks the one professor had no students. Finally a fellow by the name of Hinton James straggled up from New Hanover County. He sold his horse somewhere around Fayetteville or Sanford, and walked the rest of the way in. A university was born.

During the War for Southern Independence, units of Michigan cavalry occupied the UNC campus. They stabled their horses in the library building. This was later said to account both for the intelligence of Michigan horses and the horse sense of the Tarheel students. The general in charge of the Northern troops married the daughter of the president of the University, a nuptial match that may have contributed to the tolerant spirit for which UNC much later became famous. Under the presidency of Frank Porter Graham in the Thirties and Forties, UNC smashed the mold of Southern conservatism and actually welcomed new ideas. Over at Raleigh, 20 miles away, the state legislature reacted with spasms of heartburn and apoplexy, but the *News & Disturber* under Jonathan Daniels backed the campus radicals and liberalism triumphed. In recent years UNC has grown to house 21,000 students and 2,000 professors, some of them as preoccupied with other-worldly affairs as the professor who was accosted during the 1960 presidential campaign by a handsome woman visitor to the campus. "I'm Jack Kennedy's mother," said she. "Kennedy. Kennedy," said the professor. "I don't believe I've ever had him in one of my classes."

Off Season.
Blowing Rock, North Carolina.

Reflections of the First Baptist Church.
Integon Building; Winston-Salem, North Carolina.

High Ramparts.
Grandfather Mountain, North Carolina.

Boone from Rich Mountain.
Watauga County, North Carolina.

42

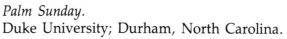

Palm Sunday.
Duke University; Durham, North Carolina.

Hydrant and Azaleas.
Raleigh, North Carolina.

Mountain Children.
Boone, North Carolina.

Asheville Rooftops.
Asheville, North Carolina.

Downtown Overview.
Raleigh, North Carolina.

December Dawn at Marshall Park.
Charlotte, North Carolina.

It's an easy drive from Winston-Salem and Greensboro south to Charlotte, where the downtown buildings sparkle and the one-way streets bewilder, and so on to Columbia. The capitol there is in the old tradition, hardly to be distinguished from capitol buildings all the way to Carson City, save for one thing: The capitol at Columbia still bears the scars of Sherman's march. Come to think of it, a sense of wars past pervades the place. There are paintings of the Revolutionary War, a monument to the Sons of South Carolina who fell in the 1847 war with Mexico, poignant reminders of the Civil War, a pedestal that once held a cannon captured at Santiago in 1898. The state takes its military history as seriously as it takes its politics, and that is very seriously indeed.

The President's House (1810).
University of South Carolina; Columbia, South Carolina.

Charleston and Savannah, Sister Cities

The fast way to get from Columbia to Charleston is by way of Interstate 26. The best way to get there is to go a little south, by way of Orangeburg and Summerville, or to go a little north and drive down by the shores of Lake Marion and Moncks Corner. Either way you get a feeling of a tempo that started a couple of centuries ago at *largo* and isn't likely ever to make it even to *andante*. You may also search again for the metaphor that stays tangled in the Spanish moss, for the moss that is so deceptively soft is stubborn stuff. It conceals the hard bare limbs of winter, just as Southern rhetoric takes the edge off ugliness. The moss makes shadows that are gentle—they are hardly shadows at all—but they are shadows all the same. The South lives with them.

Charlestonians call it the Holy City, and they delight in other small conceits. Charleston, a visitor is told, is the place "where the Ashley and the Cooper converge to form the Atlantic Ocean." A Charleston dowager once was asked if she had plans to travel. "Why go anywhere," she replied, "when you're already there?"

What makes Charleston distinctive? I put the question to Jack Leland of the *Post*. He recalled that just after World War II, *Cosmopolitan* magazine asked Somerset

Maugham to list 20 people, places, or things that had that indefinable something called "class." Maugham came up with a list that included two cities, along with such other choices as Winston Churchill, Greta Garbo, and a Jeep with a peppermint-striped canvas top. His classiest two cities in the world were San Francisco and Charleston.

Yes, Charleston has class, but it is not the kind of class that ordinarily we associate with great wealth or conspicuous excellence. This is quiet class, nothing flashy, nothing that calls attention to itself. If Charleston were buying a fine car, Charleston would buy a Bentley instead of a Rolls. Charleston is not a dozen long-stemmed roses; Charleston is a single fresh-cut camellia afloat in a crystal bowl.

You will understand that I am speaking of old Charleston, the historic district south of Calhoun Street. The rest of the metropolitan area, to be blunt about it, isn't much. Cross the two rivers, and you could be Anywhere, U.S.A. But south of Calhoun—ah, that is a different matter.

It is the intimacy of this small community that makes Charleston so special. Here the houses are snuggled as closely as spoons in a sideboard, and if here and there the paint is peeling, the brass is always shining. We paint Charleston in pastels—the houses petal pink, smoke gray, dark olive, oyster white, and the subdued and unobtrusive colors tell us something of the character of the Charlestonians who dwell within. Intimacy implies not only closeness but privacy also. The district must rank among the friendliest and most hospitable communities on earth, but Charleston is characterized also by shutters and hedges and walls. The typical house down by the Battery has two doors, one that admits a visitor to the long gallery or piazza, another that opens into the home itself.

"Gentle blood," said Spenser, "will gentle manners make." Here in Charleston, manners count for more than money. That which is left unsaid can say more than that which is said. Thirty-odd years ago a fellow of considerable wealth, the wealth having been doubtfully acquired, let it be known that his daughter would make her debut at Christmas. Nothing was said publicly—that would have been unseemly—but there was no debutante season that year. The city's oldest social organization is the St. Cecilia Society. The story is told that a new member once inquired respectfully if he might obtain for his wife a copy of the society's rules and bylaws, the better thereby to avoid inadvertent offense. He was told kindly that the St. Cecilia Society had no written rules and bylaws. His lady would be expected to know the rules that governed shoulder straps, long white gloves, and the arrangement of a proper dance card.

Today's Charleston is peculiarly a product of the city's yesterdays. Many of the yesterdays have been hard yesterdays. Long ago the seaport city trafficked darkly in the South's peculiar institution. Until outraged mariners captured the pirate Steve Bonnet in 1718, and hanged him and 38 of his crew down by the Old Exchange,

Hallowed Ground.
Trinity Episcopal Church; Columbia, South Carolina.

The Greenville County Museum of Art.
Greenville, South Carolina.

The South Caroliniana Library.
Columbia, South Carolina.

Springwood Cemetery.
Greenville, South Carolina.

Winter Sun.
Sylvan Bros. Jewelers; Columbia, South Carolina.

Main Street, December Evening.
Columbia, South Carolina.

Moody Afternoon along the Ashley.
Charleston, South Carolina.

Low Tide at Sunset.
Kiawah Island, South Carolina.

52

piracy was endemic. Often we think of the American Revolution only in terms of Massachusetts and Virginia, but South Carolina witnessed 177 clashes with the British before the war ended at Yorktown. In 1861 Charleston started the War for Southern Independence, and that war nearly ended Charleston. A Northern correspondent in 1866 found "a city of ruins, of desolation, of vacant houses, of widowed women, of rotting wharves, of deserted warehouses, of weed-wild gardens, of miles of grass-grown streets, of acres of pitiful and voiceful barrenness—that is Charleston, wherein rebellion loftily reared its head five years ago." The miseries of Reconstruction were compounded by natural disasters—an earthquake in 1886, a hurricane in 1911—and these miseries were made worse by economic hardships. Cotton, indigo and rice once provided a flourishing export trade. None survived the changes wrought by technology and time.

Yet something in the indomitable character of the people, white and black alike, forged a stronger sense of community out of the successive setbacks. The postwar poverty (post-Civil War, that is) had one pleasant consequence: Charlestonians, too poor to build new houses, continued to live in their old ones. Except for a couple of Victorian anachronisms, the district has retained its uniform antebellum charm. The geography of the peninsula contributed to a defensive solidarity. The Cooper on the east and the Ashley on the west kept the city nicely bounded. Politics played a hand. The Solid South kept sending Democrats to Congress and Charleston's Democrats stayed there forever, rising to committee chairmanships and floating bread back across the waters. Charleston's naval base today contributes mightily to the economic and social life of the city.

Much of that social life revolves around the ancient Southern pastimes of eating and drinking. Charleston prides itself not only on its she-crab soup, but on many other dishes also. The city's cuisine reflects the cosmopolitan inheritance of French, Germans, Swiss and Italians. It relies delightfully upon the natural resources of the nearby Coast. For many years following the repeal of Prohibition, South Carolina remained officially and legally dry. Most of the State, however reluctantly, observed the law. Charleston remained genteelly aloof. At a time when it was all but impossible to get even a decent glass of beer in Spartanburg, Greenville, Conway and Columbia, restaurants in the Holy City offered their customers a martini that packed a mighty wallop. Such humane ministrations were in the best Charlestonian tradition. I am told (and would not check the story for the world) that a prominent local Episcopalian annually makes his pledge not in dollars but in vintage Burgundy, and that communicants each Sunday return from the rail with renewed assurance of the splendid works of divine providence. There have been exceptions to this pleasant custom: General Francis Marion, the legendary Swamp Fox, was said to drink nothing stronger than a pint of vinegar daily, and there once was a restaurant on Meeting Street called the Teetotal. But the general is long gone and the restaurant burned

Sunday after Services.
Emanuel A.M.E. Church;
Charleston, South Carolina.

Window over Colonial Lake.
The Wagner House; Charleston, South Carolina.

Conversation at Church and Broad.
Charleston, South Carolina.

55

unmourned in the Great Fire of December, 1861. Today the cheerful clink of Charleston glasses sounds as sweetly as the song of nightingales. This is a *civilized* city.

It has known some bawdy times. Jack Leland, an authority on such matters, once undertook to compile a definitive tally of the city's houses of ill fame in 1935, but abandoned the project at a count of twenty-nine. Most of these houses were small operations, but at least one or two were said to provide a certain elegance. A young British-born rake, one Beresford, attained such fame for his patronage that the city fathers admiringly named a street after him, just off Chalmers north of Broad. It remained Beresford Lane until after World War II, when a disgusted commandant at the Naval Base served notice on the City Council: Either the houses were closed, or he would declare the entire city off limits to the fleet. That terrible threat proved so effective that the cops at once evicted the madams, and the street became Fulton Street. Things are reasonably respectable now.

A few other institutions have gone with the winds of twentieth-century change. The old Charleston Hotel, a building of architectural distinction, was torn down to make way for an absolutely abominable motel. The city's Orphan House and its chapel yielded to a Sears, and then Sears moved its store to the suburbs. But compared to other cities, Charleston has suffered little from the ravages of progress. Within the historic district, restoration is a continuing process. Soft echoes remain of the old Charleston speech. In nearby Summerville, you still hear Gullah spoken. The old family names have not gone away. For 300 years Charlestonians have watched ships come and go in their harbor, and to this day they continue to look through their window on the world. Standing on the seawall along East Bay Street, a six-year-old granddaughter of my acquaintance watches her father's ship put out to sea. She is bundled in a bright-red coat against the cool March winds, and she waves and waves until the destroyer *Pratt* is out of sight.

Firefighters.
Charleston, South Carolina.

Colonial Lake at Dusk.
Charleston, South Carolina.

59

Inbound on the Cooper River.
Charleston, South Carolina.

Light Traffic on Broad Street.
Charleston, South Carolina.

"Stiffen That Lip!"
The Citadel; Charleston, South Carolina.

Bankers Trust at Christmas.
Charleston, South Carolina.

Mixed Lighting on Meeting Street.
Charleston, South Carolina.

From Charleston to Savannah, as Delta and the seabirds fly, it's only 85 or 90 miles. Loafing along by way of Beaufort and Port Royal, the traveler finds the trip much longer—but Beaufort is worth the trouble. Anything is worth the trouble that brings a traveler to Savannah.

Anyone who has had girl children, or knows a family with girl children, knows one truth about sisters. They can be remarkably alike in some ways, and remarkably different in others. So it is with Charleston and Savannah.

Passing the Afternoon.
Charleston, South Carolina.

Battery Facade.
Charleston, South Carolina.

Catfish and Quiet.
Stone Mountain Memorial Park, Georgia.

Counting the whole of their urbanized areas, the two sister cities are about of a size. Both are seaports. Both have survived the calamities of nature and the sorrows of war. Both are cities of captivating architectural charm. Both are miserable places in the steamy days of August. Southerners who have lived in both cities are hard put to say which one they love the more.

Yet there are differences—some of them quite subtle differences—that make Charleston and Savannah quite separate entities. Charleston, which passed 300 in 1970, is older than Savannah at 250. Charleston looks outward to the sea; Savannah looks inward to its river. In some ways, Charleston has been luckier: Charleston never had to work at conservation and restoration as hard as Savannah has worked, with the result that Savannah has a younger sister's pride of special achievement. The pace in Charleston is slow, but the pace in Savannah is even slower. They call Savannah "the walking city" with good reason. In the heart of town just about everyone walks to work, sauntering through one square after another. Both cities are a bit daft about gardens and houses, but Savannah is the dafter of the two.

For all its leisurely pace, Savannah—perhaps because of her relative youth—now and then evinces a kind of gusto that one rarely senses in Charleston. You wouldn't find a really rowdy parade in Charleston—the city is a little too dignified for that— but the St. Patrick's Day Parade in Savannah has become a phenomenal event. The city flings itself into a cheerful orgy of green hats, green ties, green beer, and even, God save the mark, green grits. Some years ago some enterprising Hibernians commissioned 20 boats, each carrying a cargo of 45 gallons of green dye, and set out to turn the Savannah River green. It didn't work—the river stayed adamantly brown— but it was the spirit that counted.

The Irish shenanigans of March are echoed by Scottish festivities in November, when members of the St. Andrews Society sponsor their memorable feasts. Such is the stamina of true-blue Savannahians that on special occasions—anniversaries, birthdays, class reunions, any Saturday night—they are known to serve Chatham Artillery Punch.

I digress long enough to tell you about Chatham Artillery Punch. It is compounded in this alarming fashion: Six weeks before the special occasion aforesaid, one deposits in a large cool crock, a half-gallon of tea, the juice of nine oranges and nine lemons, a pound or so of brown sugar, and a pint of maraschino cherries. Then one anoints this inoffensive mixture with three quarts of white wine, a quart of dark rum, a quart of brandy, a quart of rye whiskey and a quart of gin. After these ingredients have had the six weeks to get acquainted with each other, to mellow and blend and run together, to talk things over, and to develop a bouquet that would fell a dray horse, the punch is pronounced almost drinkable. It is thereupon poured over a 25-pound cake of ice, and three quarts of fine champagne are then poured over *that*. Two brass buttons off a Confederate uniform are dropped in the mix. If

64

Savannah River Dawn.
Savannah, Georgia.

the buttons dissolve, it is done. Admiral George Dewey, a brave Republican, came to Savannah in 1900 and spent an evening over Chatham Artillery Punch. The next morning he announced his candidacy for President of the United States on a Democratic ticket.

That stretcher comes from the late Judge Alexander A. Lawrence, a storyteller whose reputation for deadpan, unembellished fact was known all the way from Bay Street to Broughton—a distance of about four blocks. The judge was a great kidder—he wrote a book called *Tongue in Cheek*—but his teasing usually held tidbits of truth. One evening in 1950 the Georgia Bar Association invited the Hon. Leverett Saltonstall to deliver a banquet speech. Judge Lawrence, introducing the guest, took the opportunity to remark what an encouraging sign this was for national unity. "Less than five score years after General Sherman was here, we are able to invite the senior Senator from the great Commonwealth of Massachusetts to address a Georgia audience."

In point of fact the Saltonstall dinner was only 86 years after General Sherman wrote one of the most memorable dispatches in the annals of warfare.

Savannah, Ga. Dec. 22 1864

To his Excellency,
  President Lincoln:
Dear Sir,
  I beg to present you as a Christmas Gift, the City of Savannah with 150 heavy guns and plenty of ammunition; and also about 25,000 bales of cotton.

W. T. SHERMAN
Maj. Genl.

Amber Moments.
Savannah, Georgia.

Spring Again.
Greensboro, Georgia.

Colonial Park.
Savannah, Georgia.

Shadows at Telfair Square.
Savannah, Georgia.

Class in Session.
Savannah College of Art and Design;
Savannah, Georgia.

Light on the Parapets.
Fort Pulaski National Monument;
Savannah, Georgia.

Muzzled Cannons.
Fort Pulaski National Monument; Savannah, Georgia.

When Schools Had Style.
Chatham Academy; Savannah, Georgia.

A few years earlier, a war correspondent had written of Savannah, "Probably there is no city in the Confederacy where you would be so struck by the military air that pervades everything as here." Some of this military air still lingers. A long line of palm trees—some chauvinists say the longest line of palm trees in the world—stretches out Victory Drive toward the sea. The avenue commemorates Savannah's dead of World War I.

Like her sister city of Charleston, Savannah gives great weight socially to what has gone before. I have a notion, not subject to empirical evidence, that Savannah may be even stuffier than Charleston or Richmond in this regard. It is possible for an outlander (by which is meant anyone not born in Savannah) to gain access to the inner circles, but Savannah is a difficult port of entry. Newcomers should understand that manners count, that dress is prized, that the art of understatement is admired, but that acceptance takes time. As it happens, time is what Savannahians have the most of. Their clocks strike not hours, but generations. The two questions most universally put to the young are, "What would your grandfather think?" and, "Who was his grandmother, dear?"

Many other Southern cities (and many Northern and Midwestern cities) also raise barriers to easy social acceptance. Savannah's distinction lies in a different direction. Thanks to General Oglethorpe, Savannah was born with beautiful bones. The general fashioned a skeleton city of tactically useful squares. In the event of attack, the squares would provide places of troop encampment. Around the squares he laid out neat lots for the arriving settlers. He anchored the squares with trust grants to churches. The general was a city-planning genius ahead of his time.

Savannah nearly lost the whole thing. As the decades passed, the squares began to decay and then to disappear. Three small squares on Montgomery Street were cut in two. Ellis Square, once the scene of a colorful city market, fell to aesthetic vandals who built a parking garage on the site. That piece of destruction was too much for a prominent citizen, Mills B. Lane. He went into action, rallied the ladies of Savannah, and before long the Historic Savannah Foundation was born. In the field of urban restoration, nothing has surpassed the success story of Savannah. More than a thousand homes and buildings have been restored. Most of the houses are occupied by residents who work in the area. Others have been converted to law offices, architects' offices, doctors' offices and the like. Most cities die at night, when daytime occupants retreat to the suburbs. Not Savannah. The squares and their connecting streets stay alive in the evenings. By day the inner city delights the eye. Savannah is leaf-dappled in autumn, ablaze with roses and azaleas through the long spring. Here fountains of azaleas grow, filling the yards, splashing onto the streets.

Maggie Ledford Lawson, who did much of the research for this essay, lived for several years in Savannah. She fell in love with the place. In some ways, she found,

Savannah is a city of ghosts, of shadows at high noon. It is a city with the character of an ageless elegant woman, flirting with grandeur behind a fan of ironwork. It is a lotus land: "People come to Savannah planning to stay a year or two. At first they think it's nothing special. They find the city inbred, provincial. But Savannah is the ultimate seductress. Once you've lived here, you're ruined for anywhere else. If you go away, determined to put Savannah behind, the memory follows you. By comparison any other place is flat, dull, mediocre. Savannah weaves a web of human relationships, one generation connected to another, strands of love knotted to strands of hatred, the whole forming an almost invisible linkage of past and present. The squares are the metaphor. We move from Ellis Square to Telfair Square to Wright Square to Johnson Square, chess amid the roses, allegory in the walkways. Place and people merge, but the place always holds ultimate dominion, for the place endures."

Bright Afternoon.
Savannah, Georgia.

The Finishing Touches.
Savannah, Georgia.

Early One Sunday.
Telfair Square; Savannah, Georgia.

71

Running before the Storm.
St. Marys Channel. Georgia.

Estuarine Waters.
Coastal Georgia.

Silhouette of an Old City.
St. Augustine, Florida.

Moonrise.
St. Augustine, Florida.

75

These Were the 'Palmy' Days

Southouth of Savannah, the highway leads down through Brunswick to Jacksonville, and I pause long enough to say a word about Jacksonville's public schools and Jacksonville's newspapers. Both institutions are first-rate. The city itself is a most attractive city—not as historic as St. Augustine—but a fine place to live and raise children. St. Augustine is red-tiled roofs and oyster walls, crisp shadows on the courtyard of the Castillo de San Marcos, sundials and anniversary watches, old couples arm in arm.

We are driving through mile after mile of condos and beach motels and a million fried chickens down to Daytona Beach—*vrooom!*—and then over to Orlando to see what's new at Disney World. What's new is the amazing growth. Orlando won't stop; it won't even slow down. Back on the Coast, things are quieter at Canaveral than they used to be in the great days of space shots, but the occasional launchings have lost none of their fascination.

We mosey along the Boulevard de la Tastee-Freeze, through beaches and boats and bathing suits, wondering if anyone in Vero Beach ever eats at home, and so to Stuart. Nothing distinctive here, but a good town—a town with a smile on its face. Finally a sign on the turnpike gives notice. Destination reached. Palm Beach.

It all began, this combination of fantasy and fact and fiction, when a Civil War draft dodger, name of Lang, built a hut on an island off the Florida coast. This was in 1862. For a few years he farmed by himself, but then the place got crowded. By 1873 the population had swelled to eight. Some historians say ten. There were thought to be nineteen families there on a January day in 1878 when the Spanish brigantine *Providencia* ran aground in Lake Worth. The captain had a cargo of wine and coconuts. Someone said, "Let's have a beach party," which is what someone always is saying in Florida, and after the party the captain departed for parts unknown. The whole thing may have been an insurance scam. Anyhow, he left the coconuts behind.

Two other fellows, names of Hammon and Lainhart, were capitalists of the old school. They claimed the coconuts and sold them for two and a half cents each. Theirs was the art of making something out of nothing, which is always a nice trick if you can bring it off. When their fellow settlers had nothing better to do, they all planted coconuts. They wound up by planting 14,000 coconuts. As time went on, they gazed upon their handiwork and found it good. That was how Palm Beach was born, a *piña colada* of a place, sired by a few free-booting fellows who knew how to seize an opportunity when it washed up on the shore. They were men with time on their hands and a vision of the good life.

The next such fellow to come along was Henry Morrison Flagler in 1893. Flagler had discovered St. Augustine in 1883, some 300 years after the Spanish had discovered it first, but the Spanish had done nothing much with the property and Flagler knew a good thing when he saw it. He built two fabulous hotels and bought a third one. He built a railway. Then he got bored with St. Augustine, which is not hard to do, especially if you're 63 years old and have a keen mind and a hundred million dollars getting restless in your pocket. He came south another 200 miles and saw those 14,000 palm trees. He said, this is a great place to make another ten or twenty million dollars, and it will be more fun than Standard Oil.

So he built hotels in Palm Beach, fabulous hotels, first the Royal Poinciana and then the Palm Beach Inn—this was the first Breakers—and he built a railway to bring the rich and famous to Palm Beach where they could play games with the rich and famous. They came at Christmas and they departed after the George Washington Ball on February 22. These were the Goulds and Wanamakers and Astors and Vanderbilts. Some of the guests came in their own yachts. Pierre Lorillard had a yacht so large that he kept Jersey cows on board to provide milk for his friends. One of the other regulars had a yacht so large that the lifeboats had lifeboats. No one was amazed at such opulence. Didn't everyone have a yacht?

Flagler was born in 1830. He had a first wife, and after a time he had a second wife, name of Alice, and in 1901 he took a third wife, name of Mary Lily. The circumstances are interesting. In 1896, at the age of 48, Alice went bonkers. The

78

doctors called it "incurable chronic delusional insanity," and so it was. She developed a crush on Nicholas II, czar of all the Russias, and believed she was corresponding with him. The czar was then 28, a bit young. He would be deposed. The same thing would happen to Alice.

While Alice was in New York, dreaming of her czar, husband Henry was living it up in Florida. Henry was a handsome dawg. He had met Mary Lily in 1891, during his St. Augustine period. He was 61. She was 24, a bit young. She sang to him. Millionaires are only mortal, after all. When it became apparent that Alice would never recover from Nicholas II, Flagler acted with the boldness that had made him so rich. On April 9, 1901, he arranged for a bill to be introduced in the Florida State Senate, providing for divorce on grounds of incurable insanity. Ten days later the bill had passed both houses. On April 25 the governor, name of Jennings, signed it into law. In June Flagler filed for divorce. In August the divorce was granted. On August 21, he announced his engagement to Mary Lily. On August 24 they wed. Alice never knew a thing about all this. Henry saw that she had a settlement of $2 million; she was cared for happily to the end of her days in 1930. The law was repealed in 1905.

Old Henry and young Mary Lily were blissful. She wanted a big house. He built her a four-million-dollar mansion, name of Whitehall, with a magnificent pipe organ and a Louis XV ballroom in white and gold. The ballroom measured 91 by 37 feet. I do not know how many servants it took to staff the place. Lots.

While all this was going on, another handsome dawg arrived in Palm Beach. This was Colonel Edward R. Bradley. At various times he had been a steelworker, a dishwasher, a cowboy, a miner, an Indian scout, a real estate salesman, and a bookie. What he was, was a gambling man. In 1898 he established his Beach Club in Palm Beach. He was in a class with the fellows who went down to the grounded *Providencia*. He too knew coconuts when he saw them. Until shortly before his death in 1946, the colonel ran an impeccable casino. It was all illegal, of course, but when big money flashes, the law blinks. Bradley's was raided only once, in 47 years. It was an accident.

The colonel allowed no drinking on the floor, but he spread a superlative table. To this day Palm Beach is full of aging high rollers who profess to remember the green turtle soup. The colonel had rules. After 6 o'clock, it was black tie for the gentlemen and long dresses for the ladies, and he brooked no violations. Walter Chrysler once spent an afternoon at roulette. Came the witching hour and he remained in his seat. The proprietor touched the Chrysler elbow.

"I can't quit now," said the eminent tycoon, "I'm down $20,000."

"I will flip you a coin," said the colonel. "Double or nothing." He flipped a silver dollar, slapped it on his wrist, and instantly put the dollar away. "You win," he said.

"You never even looked at it," protested Chrysler.

"Walter," said the colonel, "go home and get properly dressed."

Gambling was a way of life in Palm Beach. One wealthy fellow, a candyman, name of Loft, came down from New York and asked if he could join a friendly game. He had never been in Palm Beach before. Welcome, he was told. He inquired about the stakes. Table stakes, they said. He put $10,000 on the table. They gave him one chip. Another tale involves one of the Woolworth ladies. A few days after the death of her husband, a regular at Bradley's, she telephoned to ask if he had left any debt unpaid. The colonel demurred. He would not think of pressing the matter. It was nothing. The lady insisted and at last the colonel looked up the gentleman's marker: $150,000. He had her check the next day. Another widow, suddenly bereft, was amazed to find that her late husband had left her $40 million. She couldn't resist talking about her good fortune. The colonel quietly shushed her. "Don't mention it," he advised. "They wouldn't think much of $40 million down here."

The colonel lived by his own rules and died by his own rules. He left orders that on his death the club was to be demolished and a public park established in its place. So it was, and it is Bradley Park to this day. Old Joe Kennedy, a longtime resident of Palm Beach, mourned its passing. "When Bradley's went," he said, "this place lost its zipperoo."

These were the palmy days. Year after year the Palm Beach *Daily News* chronicled the arrivals, the parties, the departures of the great names: Dodge, Duke, Cromwell, Hutton, McCormick, Guggenheim, Rockefeller, Phipps. There wasn't yet a Sixteenth Amendment. The sea was blue and the sand was beige, and Palm Beach was a gorgeous meringue. Dolly Martin promenaded down the Poinciana's Peacock Alley with diamonds in the heels of her shoes. C.W. Barron, founder of *Barron's Weekly*, came for the season bringing five tuxedos with him. Every two weeks, he moved up to the next size larger. In March he went to Sarasota Springs to sweat it all off.

In 1918 the next great character came along. This was Addison Mizner, born in California in 1872. Before he saw the coconuts, he had been a prospector in the Klondike, a prizefighter in Australia, a collector of antiques, a student of architecture, and not to put too fine a point upon it, a looter of cathedrals in Spain and Guatemala. He bought candelabra, altars, statues, lavabos, church furnishings, anything he could get his hands on. He figured they would come in handy some day, and he was right.

In 1917 Mizner fell in with Paris Singer. He was another handsome dawg, a blond full-bearded fellow, one of the many sons of Isaac Merit Singer, the sewing machine man. Paris Singer is variously described as an artist, an architect, a scientist, and a lover; he had a tempestuous affair with Isadora Duncan. At the moment, he was bored.

Mizner was not a handsome dawg. He weighed 300 pounds and had trouble getting around. The two hit it off. Mizner had ideas and Singer had money. They proposed to build a convalescent hospital for the veterans who would soon be coming home. Then they had a better idea: They would convert the hospital into a club; they would call it the Everglades Club, and they would make it so exclusive that the rich would be panting for admission. Exactly so. Singer ran the place in autocratic fashion; he alone was the membership committee.

Mizner wanted to build houses—great houses, houses with arches and courtyards and minarets, houses with gardens and balconies and cloisters, houses with columns and fountains and pools. The rich were waiting for him. Mrs. E.T. Stotesbury saw the Everglades Club. She wanted something along the same lines. Mizner built El Mirasol for her. It had only 37 rooms before she started adding on, but it had some nice touches—a private zoo, housing for 50 servants, an underground garage for 40 cars, a reception lounge for visitors' chauffeurs. Some mean-spirited critic said spitefully that Mizner forgot to include a kitchen, but it wasn't so; he provided a splendid kitchen, thoughtfully located downwind from the dining rooms. Here Mrs. Stotesbury reigned for more than twenty years. They called her Queen Eva.

Mizner built other great houses—Playa Riente for Joshua Cosden, Casa Bendita for John Phipps. He gave them vaulted ceilings and beamed ceilings and ceilings with frescoes. He designed white exteriors and red-tiled roofs, and he adorned these houses with candelabra, altars, statues, and lavabos, because he had known they would come in handy some day. When he ran out of the real things, he established a factory over in West Palm to reproduce them. When he was casting stone stairs, he had a workman walk in hobnailed boots over the stairs before they set, the better to give the effect of the spurs of Spanish grandees. All of this may have been "ersatz Hispano-Mooresque," as Ada Louise Huxtable complained in *The New York Times*, but the customers loved it.

Palm Beach in the Twenties was rich, rich, rich. Even after the market collapsed on Black Tuesday 1929, some of the high rollers kept rolling. Marjorie Merriweather Post first came to Palm Beach in 1909. In 1923, when she was Mrs. Edward P. Hutton, she set out to build a spread that would wipe Mrs. Stotesbury's eye. The result was Mar-a-Lago, a modest castle of 115 rooms on South Ocean Boulevard. To the east was the ocean, reached by her own tunnel beneath the roadway; to the west was Lake Worth. In between were seventeen acres of lawns and gardens and a nine-hole par-three golf course. Mrs. Post had a 75-foot tower; in the tower was a blue spotlight to provide a blue moon for parties. She gave great parties. Guests arrived in an entrance hall tiled with Fourteenth-Century tiles. They proceeded to a living room with a 36-foot ceiling. If the winter evenings were cool, a fireplace provided warmth; the fireplace took six-foot logs. Beyond the living room was the main dining room. On intimate occasions, guests sat at a twelve-foot marble table, inlaid with semi-precious stones. The table was made for her in Florence. On larger occasions, it could be expanded to twenty-nine feet. She personally saw to it that the gold plates were centered precisely sixteen inches apart. Opposite the dining room was a room called the library. It had magnificent paneling, but it held only 84 books. The house went on and on. The kitchens were hotel-sized, and a good thing, too, for Mrs. Post had a way of inviting 300 or 400 guests at a time. Once she hired the Ringling Brothers Circus to perform on the lawn. Sometimes she brought her friends to Palm Beach on her yacht; this was the *Sea Cloud*, sixteen feet longer than a football field. Sometimes she flew them down to Florida in her four-engined plane. They came, and they looked upon Mar-a-Lago, and they marveled. Most of them marveled. Addison Mizner took one look at the place. "My God," he cried, "Harry Thaw shot the wrong architect."

Mrs. Post, a first-rate businesswoman, kept a close eye on her wealth. Others never knew how rich they were. One of the Philadelphia Donner girls, then about 18, once was driving home from Palm Beach. She telephoned for a reservation at the Mayflower Hotel in Washington and on arrival was escorted by the manager to a sumptuous suite. The young lady protested that she was short on cash and wanted nothing so fancy, but the manager insisted. A day or so later, at a family dinner back home in Philadelphia, she renewed her complaint. Her uncle, who served as a financial adviser to the family, took her aside for a chat in the library.

"My dear," he said, "you're a big girl now, and there are some things you really should know. For example, among other things, you *own* the Mayflower."

This is another Palm Beach story: Forty-odd years ago, sorrow struck the household of a wealthy fellow, name of Searles. His wife died. The bereaved widower proposed to build a magnificent mausoleum in her memory and commissioned an architect to prepare a suitable design. The architect came up with a design so unspeakably gaudy—so replete with cherubs, angels, columns, arches, porticos and gazebos—that the Town Council refused to waive its rule against tombs in Palm Beach. Months passed while the matter was bartered back and forth. Meanwhile the lady lay on ice. The widower at last abandoned the project and then completely forgot about his late lamented. The mortuary kept sending bills to the gentleman's trust fund at Manufacturers Hanover; the trustees paid the bills, and the lady stayed on ice. Some years later, when the fellow was going through divorce from his next wife, all this came out in the press. "It just slipped my mind," he explained.

Palm Beach has known some interesting trials for divorce. Mary Alice Sullivan married Russell Firestone in 1961. They separated in 1964. Three years later, after a spectacular trial, he was granted a divorce, but the trial judge scolded both of them for extra-marital affairs. "The big trouble," said the judge, "was total incapacity on the part of either for domestication." A stringer for *Time* magazine had trouble understanding the court's opinion; the misunderstanding led to a libel suit; the libel suit led to the Supreme Court's opinion on March 2, 1976, in *Time, Inc.* v. *Mary Alice Firestone*, 424 US 448, one of the most significant decisions of recent years in the field of libel law. Justice Rehnquist, speaking for a five-man majority, held that Mary Alice was not a "public figure," a holding almost as bizarre as the case itself. Who could flow in the mainstreams of Palm Beach and not be a public figure?

Well, not much remains of the high life that developed with Flagler and Bradley and Mizner. After the stockmarket crash, Mizner made a stab at building new castles in Boca Raton, but nothing much came of the venture and he died in 1933. During the depression, a writer for *Fortune* magazine painted a melancholy picture of Palm Beach in the winter season. Here live "some of the most weary, restless, spendthrift people to be found gathered in one spot in North America. They constitute a segment of the international society which gives allegiance to nothing except wealth. Their origins are various: They come from Philadelphia, London, what was Petrograd, Rome, Madrid. They are as irresponsible as savages and not half so contented. They whirl and eddy, marry and remarry, so inextricably mingled that you can tell one family from another only by the sound of its name on scandal-worn tongues."

I asked Judge James R. Knott about all this. Judge Knott, a longtime resident, is the historian emeritus and plenipotentiary of Palm Beach. He is among the most amiable and generous men of all time. He fed me all the tales I have been telling, and I added a little embroidery of my own. He says that whatever truth may have been contained in the *Fortune* article, the image of 1936 bears small resemblance to Palm Beach today. True, families of great wealth still come to Palm Beach, and many of them live there for most of the year, but the era of conspicuous frivolity is long gone. Today's residents are a quiet lot, good citizens, active in local charities, not especially eager to be photographed for the shiny-sheeted *Daily News*.

Nothing quite like Palm Beach exists anywhere in the South, or anywhere else for that matter. The town is immaculate, largely because crews constantly clean up the fallen palm branches and see that trash is collected five days a week. There still are no funeral parlors in the town, and no resident plumbers; these necessary trades are plied across the water in West Palm. No line of laundry may be hung publicly in Palm Beach, for laundry is not a matter to be publicly discussed. The population swells in the winter season, when the number of Rolls-Royces on Worth Avenue seems to double, but the extreme fluctuations have ended. Month in and month out, the beautiful people—and some not so beautiful—dwell peacefully in their whipped-cream little city, bleached by sun and idleness, seeing the good life through amber glasses, recognizing as always good coconuts when they see them.

Promenade on the St. Johns.
Jacksonville, Florida.

Casablanca of the South

South of Palm Beach the condos rise, all in a line down highway A1A, files on review, their glass eyes fixed above the endless traffic down below. Fort Lauderdale is blue water and white sails, where time is kept by pendulum masts along the trim canals. Hollywood is glistening skin and suntan oil, deckchairs by the big pool of the Diplomat Hotel, convention badges: Hi! My name's Jerry. The presidential suite at the Diplomat used to have a notice on the back of its door that set forth the minimum rates: $750 a night, every extra guest $11. The walls of the suite were done in carpeting of red and orange and purple. Just like the song says, that's Hollywood.

Miami is a puzzle, a sprawling enigma of a city. Over on the Beach, a frequent visitor finds few changes year by year. Some of the hotels are ticky-tack, some are posh as petits fours in a bakery shop. The same tourists sit on the same bus stop benches, the same limousines swim as smoothly as sea trout through swarms of tropical fish. The Beach survives on conventions, and after some lean years and some bad experiences, the conventions are returning. Thousands of permanent residents live here, but the Beach clings to a sense of passive expectancy; it is a suitcase half unpacked, waiting to be packed again.

Metered Sand.
Clearwater Beach, Florida.

Beachfront Congestion.
Gulf Boulevard; Clearwater Beach, Florida.

Florida-by-the-Sea.
Clearwater Beach, Florida.

87

American Egret.
Everglades National Park, Florida.

Gulls in Flight.
Anastasia State Recreation Area, Florida.

The Don CeSar.
St. Petersburg Beach, Florida.

Cervantes Revisited.
The Siboney (detail).

The Siboney.
Ybor City; Tampa, Florida.

Rigging and Tropical Sunset.
H.M.S. *Bounty* Exhibit; St. Petersburg, Florida.

Rainy Day along the Hillsborough.
Tampa, Florida.

91

It is the city of Miami that fascinates; it attracts and repels; it divides and multiplies. This is a city 42 percent Latin, 41 percent non-Latin white, 17 percent black. It is one city, it is three cities. It might have been cloned from Los Angeles—tendon freeways, toothless skyline—but it is unlike Los Angeles. It might have been cloned from Havana, but Havana retains a certain unity. There is not much unity in Miami. The Spanish community includes Cubans, Brazilians, Colombians, Argentinians; the black community includes native-born American Negroes, Jamaicans, Haitians, Bahamians descended from the Bahamians Henry Flagler brought in to build his hotels and railroad. The white population embraces a little of everything else—old-timers, new arrivals, solid citizens, drifters, junkies. None of the factions gets along especially well with any other faction, yet the city pulses with a mysterious vitality all its own.

Part of the mystery comes from the criminal traffic in drugs. In recent years Miami has become the Casablanca of the South, the center of a commerce unimaginably vast. Here deals are cut and throats are cut. Like maggots in rotten meat, conspiracies breed within conspiracies, and the "square grouper"—the bale of marijuana—is traded on an underground exchange. Murder holds no novelty in Miami, but few of the murders make news in the *Herald*; most of the murders are drug-related, mere business risks. Murder comes with the job.

Miami is Casablanca. It is Paris and Geneva also, where wealthy South Americans and their doe-eyed wives fly in like migrant birds, he to take care of his banking, she to shop for clothes and jewels and furnishings. The city is multilingual. In Little Havana a shop window advises, *Aqui se habla Yiddish.* In a neutral park, the "No Picknicking" signs are in English, Spanish, and Hebrew. For 60,000 Latin subscribers, the Miami *Herald* is *El Herald*. The politician, merchant, lawyer, doctor, or newspaper reporter who speaks only English or only Spanish has a problem.

I never know what to make of Miami and Dade County. It matches New York in its contrasts of opulence and poverty, its extremes of friendliness and hostility, its energy and its lassitude. Whenever I look at the city, I look into the unrevealing dark mirrors of a stranger's sunglassed face. There is nothing there—and yet there is.

South of Miami lie the keys, stretching in a necklace of islands and causeways from Key Largo to Key West: fishing tackle and fishing boats and places with bait for sale. The keys are at once fragile and strong; they are terribly vulnerable to the elements, but they have grappled with the elements and the keys have survived. Key West remains a cheerful symbol of the land of the free and the home of the brave; it is a haven for the tolerantly unconventional nomads, young and old, who gather here, and it is the home of the treasure hunters and salvage crews who gamble their lives for Spanish gold. There is a nice geometry about the place: on the plane of the sea, masts perpendicular and sails triangular and winds diagonal. It's not easy to reach Key West, but the rewards are worth the effort.

Back toward Miami, then, and so across the Everglades to Naples and up the Gulf Coast to Fort Myers and Sarasota—nice town, Sarasota, with its Ringling Museum and its splendid concert hall. The pleasantest cities in Florida are St. Petersburg and Tampa, with Lakeland, Clearwater and Bradenton thrown in to boot. Good newspapers, a first-rate airport, vigorous civic spirit, a sense of caring for its people—the area has much to offer. Gainesville means a lively university, and Tallahassee means a busy capital when the legislature is in session. Nothing here is lazy. Pensacola means the Navy and Mobile means Southern seaport. One of these years, if the Tenn-Tom waterway produces the coal exports its sponsors dream of, Mobile could mean big Southern seaport. The economic benefits might restore Biloxi and Gulfport and Pass Christian to some of their old grace and elegance.

Sarasota Old and New.
Sarasota, Florida.

Where Wealth Reigned: The Old Tampa Bay Hotel.
Tampa, Florida.

City Hall Plaza.
Tampa, Florida.

Moorish Splendor: The Old Tampa Bay Hotel.
Tampa, Florida.

Beach Cabanas.
Indian Rocks Beach, Florida.

Tranquil Morning.
Indian Rocks Beach, Florida.

Ritual under the Palms.
Clearwater Beach, Florida.

To Sea and Be Seen.
Lido Beach; Sarasota, Florida.

Freedom of the Press.
St. Petersburg, Florida.

"Eternal Father. . . ."
U.S. Naval Academy Chapel; Annapolis, Maryland.

San Ysleta Mission (Corpus Christi de la Ysleta del Sur, 1682).
Ysleta, Texas.

Nave.
National Shrine of the Immaculate Conception; Washington, D.C.

St. Helena's Episcopal Church (1712).
Beaufort, South Carolina.

Wesley Plainstyle.
Watkinsville Methodist Church; Watkinsville, Georgia.

Books of Worship.
Trinity Episcopal Church (1814); Columbia, South Carolina.

St. Johannes Lutheran Church.
Charleston, South Carolina.

Downtown Presbyterian Church (1851).
Nashville, Tennessee.

acred Heart Catholic Church (1903).
Galveston, Texas.

Stained Glass Ceiling.
The Chapel of Thanksgiving; Dallas, Texas.

Children at Catechism.
Mission San Elizario; San Elizario, Texas.

ogwood Gothic.
rankfort, Kentucky.

The Healing Hands.
The City of Faith; Tulsa, Oklahoma.

An Historic Aisle.
St. John's Episcopal Church (1854);
Montgomery, Alabama.

101

Nous ne sommes pas pressés

What does New Orleans mean? I would find a metaphor in the river that cradles the city—a river at once passionate and placid, caring and indifferent, seductive and ominous. The river has a rhythm of its own, the muddy water lapping at piers and pilings, the grey-winged gliding gulls incessantly barnstorming over the waterfront. The river has been there a long time; it has carried on its broad breast the commerce of a hundred flags; in beetle trains the barges slowly come and slowly go, but the current is swifter than it looks. The river is deceptive. So is this city.

No one can write about New Orleans without writing of the Vieux Carré and Mardi Gras, but let me touch them only lightly. The enduring enchantment of the French Quarter lies in its authenticity. How the Quarter has managed to hold onto its essential character I cannot say. I can only marvel. It is a character shaped and refined over two and a half centuries by French nobles and jazz pianists, by priests and nuns and go-go dancers, by merchants and artists and sailors—and through some miracle, seven million tourists a year haven't spoiled it. It still is possible to spend a reverent hour in the old cathedral that mothers Jackson Square and then to emerge into the rampageous color of the Square itself. The sellers of costly antiques coexist happily with the sellers of tee-shirts and bawdy postcards. Nobody ever has had to *restore* the Quarter in the way in which Memphis proposes to *restore* Beale Street, for the Quarter has an eternal life of its own. The stripteasers quit at four in the morning, and the bells toll for Mass at six.

Carnival endures in the same way. After all these years one might suppose the krewes would weary of their revelry, but it never seems to happen. It tells us something of the nature of this city that so many busy men and women, having jobs to tend to and professions to serve and households to manage, should devote such time and money to their single fleeting hour in Carnival. There is a touch of mockery here—mockery of the sober, strait-laced, nine-to-five values of a Richmond or Birmingham or Jackson. Who could imagine Mardi Gras in Dallas? No way. Dallas has more important things to do with its time and money. Big D is into banks and bonds and boardrooms, the stuff that dividends are made on. New Orleans is into floats and fluff and fantasy—into cloud-capp'd towers, gorgeous palaces and faded insubstantial pageantry that leaves no rack behind. It is just as Prospero said. This is such stuff as dreams are made on.

There's more to New Orleans than the Vieux Carré and the parades of Mardi Gras. This is a city that lists in its directory twenty-nine pages of restaurants, among them twenty-five Burger Kings and twenty-four McDonalds. It offers Brennan's, Antoine's and Galatoire's—and it offers the Cajun Catfish House as well. I don't know that New Orleans is any boozier than any other seaport city—Baltimore, for instance—but it often seems that way. Back in the Nineteenth Century, a humane law required that every prisoner in the New Orleans city jail be provided a gill of whiskey a day. There used to be a local distillation called Strip and Go Naked Gin. New Orleans dearly loves its toddy.

The city loves its old neighborhoods and street names also. Other cities are content with such pedestrian streets as Oak, Maple, Elm and Main. New Orleans has its own Willow, Walnut and Pine, to be sure, but the city also winks an eye at the classics—among its streets are Clio, Erato, Thalia, Melpomene, Terpsichore, Euterpe and Polymnia. Nobody else could be so amused by the muses. This is a city fond of music. At one time they had "spasm bands" here, long antedating the rock groups of our own time, and the old bands had great names: The Family Haircut, and the Warm Gravy. New Orleans wears its past with a feather in its cap. On All Souls Day, they picnic in the cemeteries. They open the magnificent old houses—the Pitot House, the Cizik House, the Gallier House—but New Orleans is casual about these things. You will find more peeling paint in one block along Prytania than you'll find in the whole of Charleston's Battery. New Orleans will paint its piazza tomorrow, or after Lent, or whenever really important company is coming. Meanwhile, have a glass of cool white wine, and observe the ivory petals of a flowering magnolia. The city's unwritten motto speaks for past and present: *Nous ne sommes pas pressés.* No rush.

The General and His Supporters.
Jackson Square; New Orleans, Louisiana.

The Last of a Breed.
The St. Charles Line; New Orleans, Louisiana.

107

Style in Stone: The Maritime Building.
New Orleans, Louisiana.

Blues at Dusk.
New Orleans, Louisiana.

Greenwood Cemetery.
New Orleans, Louisiana.

Summer Evening, The Vieux Carré.
New Orleans, Louisiana.

St. Charles Avenue.
New Orleans, Louisiana.

Storm over the Mississippi.
New Orleans, Louisiana.

Shipping on the Move.
New Orleans, Louisiana.

To remember Baton Rouge is to remember Huey Long and the colorful politicians so characteristic of Louisiana. To remember Alexandria, by contrast, is to remember a wildlife refuge surprisingly nearby. The most memorable thing about Natchitoches, recalled from a visit there some years ago, is being taught how to pronounce the unpronounceable name of the place. You are urged to remember that it is not pronounced Natch-i-toch-es, as in catchy-coaches. The name kind of rhymes with a bag-a-buck, but not exactly. On up the road is Shreveport, memorable chiefly for Ernest's Supper Club, the domain of one of the world's great restaurateurs, name of Ernest Palmisano. He started you out with a platter of crab claws in an oil and vinegar sauce. He continued with a shrimp cocktail made not in Louisiana but in heaven, and this was followed by flaming crab soup and red fish with lump crabmeat up top. When I ate there in 1975, his restaurant was at 516 Commerce Street. After a fire it moved to number 612, but the traditions moved with it. I have had some superlative meals in unexpected places—Bern's Steak House in Tampa and the Inn at Little Washington, Virginia—but one evening at Ernest's in Shreveport provides a memory for a lifetime.

Memphis is working on its Beale Street neighborhood, in an effort to bring back a touch of the old days, but at this writing Memphis has a long way to go. For homegrown music, the place to go in Tennessee forever will be Nashville, home of the Grand Ole Opry. The city is big in publishing, and big in insurance, but what makes Nashville famous is the Nashville sound.

If it weren't for the license plates, the Alabama accents, and the shared affection for Bear Bryant, a traveler might doubt that Birmingham and Montgomery were in the same state. Birmingham is a muscular city, built of iron and steel; it has a topnotch medical center and some attractive civic amenities, but it's more of a sister to Pittsburgh than it is to Montgomery. The capital has its strengths also, but these are political strengths and historical strengths. All capital cities have something indefinable in common—it may be the invisible electricity of political power—but if I were filming a movie on Southern politics, I'd go to Montgomery rather than to Jackson, say, or to Columbia or Frankfort.

Atlanta has grown so large that its political role gets overwhelmed by everything else. As Southern cities go, it's a young city—a big little sister who isn't even 150 years old—but it has known a hard life. By the time General Sherman departed, his troops had destroyed 3,400 of the city's 3,800 buildings. Some sections of Atlanta were so dreadfully ravaged that when spring came in 1865, no birds appeared. Smallpox made the city's misery even deeper. Survivors looked like scarecrows, with persimmon seeds for buttons and hats made of corn shucks.

Atlanta rose from its ashes. The *Constitution*, founded in 1868, provided leadership through Henry W. Grady's insistent calls for a "New South." He was no agrarian. Grady was a city boy to the core. He wanted industry. He wanted modern transportation, and before his death in 1889 he had set in motion the forces that would mold a great city. These days the Confederate memories are as faded as old battle flags, and little remains that is distinctively Southern. The city is a cosmopolitan city of many faces—the face of the black South, the face of Syrians and Irish, of Orthodox Jew and fundamentalist Baptist. It is the destination of the convention goer, the home base of the pot and pan salesman, the headquarters of great corporations, and the haven of those patient fans who root for the Falcons and the Braves.

Knoxville also knew the ravages of siege warfare, but Knoxville was smaller and luckier than Atlanta. In the 1880s, the city was little more than a whistle stop for steamers on the Tennessee River. The notion that Knoxville would one day play host to a world's fair would have seemed preposterous. But the city—and indeed the whole of East Tennessee—may have changed more remarkably than any other part of the South in the past fifty years. The area still is characterized by the oldtime religion—roadside signs still proclaim that "Jesus Saves," and teetotalers still outnumber the whiskey-drinking folks—but Oak Ridge and TVA have moved Knoxville into a new age. The 1982 Fair was an astonishingly audacious venture for a city of 185,000. And because municipal audacity is a commodity always in short supply, Knoxville merits a special salute.

For an unusually pretty drive, a traveler should take Interstate 75 up to Lexington, one of the nicest cities in the land—bluegrass and white board fences and beautiful horses at pasture—and then drive on to Louisville. Partly because of the *Courier-Journal*, the city has accepted social change with grace and good manners, and on Derby Day the city flies its fleur-de-lis flag over a sporting event that transcends all ethnic and social divisions.

113

At Anchor.
Baton Rouge, Louisiana.

In Session.
The State Capitol; Baton Rouge, Louisiana.

114

Noontime on Milam Street.
Shreveport, Louisiana.

Wendy Ruiz.
Chalmette National Historical Park;
Arabi, Louisiana.

There Must Be a Mockingbird.
Shreveport, Louisiana.

Matched Cadillacs at Tealwood.
Shreveport, Louisiana.

The Arlington Hotel.
Shreveport, Louisiana.

Jesuit vs. Mansfield.
Shreveport, Louisiana.

A Settled Sort of Place.
Belhaven; Jackson, Mississippi.

Insurance and Assurance.
The Lamar Life Building and St. Andrews Cathedral; Jackson, Mississippi.

Newsroom Consultation.
The Clarion-Ledger; Jackson, Mississippi.

Belleau Wood to Château-Thierry.
The Mississippi War Memorial; Jackson, Mississippi.

Gulf Tidal Flats.
Pass Christian, Mississippi.

The Sharpshooter.
Wisconsin Monument; Vicksburg National Military Park, Mississippi.

Wealth as Tradition.
The Mississippi Bank; Jackson, Mississippi.

A Most Satisfactory Spring.
Natchez, Mississippi.

Early Morning Soccer.
Overton Park; Memphis, Tennessee.

"Where the Delta Begins."
The Peabody Hotel; Memphis, Tennessee.

River Traffic at Sunset.
The Memphis-Arkansas Bridge; Memphis, Tennessee.

Calm Waters.
Memphis, Tennessee.

Under the Big Top.
Memphis State University,
Tennessee.

Pom-Pom Frenzy.
Memphis State University, Tennessee.

September Saturday—Southern Style.
Memphis State University, Tennessee.

130

Interstate 40 and Danny Thomas Boulevard.
Memphis, Tennessee.

132

Working the Garden.
Buntontown, Tennessee.

Public Square at Evening.
Nashville, Tennessee.

Golden Afternoon.
Centennial Park; Nashville, Tennessee.

October at Travellers' Rest.
Nashville, Tennessee.

Downtown Landmark:
The Nashville Arcade.
Nashville, Tennessee.

Main Entrance: The Western Civilization Building.
Vanderbilt University; Nashville, Tennessee.

Autumn Dawn.
Radnor Lake State Natural Area; Nashville, Tennessee.

139

Church Street.
Nashville, Tennessee.

140

Quiet Evening on Campus.
George Peabody College for Teachers; Nashville, Tennessee.

Goldenrod at the Fence Line.
Carver Gap; Roan Mountain Scenic Area, Tennessee.

The Belle of Louisville (detail).
Louisville, Kentucky.

Louisville and the George Rogers Clark Bridge.
Kentucky.

143

Urbanity with Style:
St. James Court.
Louisville, Kentucky.

Renewal and Restoration.
West Main Street;
Louisville, Kentucky.

Freeman Acres.
Mercer County, Kentucky.

The Attendant's Booth.
Frankfort, Kentucky.

Rainy Morning at the Singing Bridge.
Frankfort, Kentucky.

147

City Leaf Crew at Work.
Catalpa Road; Lexington, Kentucky.

South Mill Street.
Lexington, Kentucky.

As American as A. P.
Frankfort, Kentucky.

Gray Chill and White Fence Lines.
Kentucky Horse Park; Lexington, Kentucky.

Watercarved Riverbed.
Little Pigeon River;
Great Smoky Mountains
National Park, Tennessee.

Sycamores along the Lane.
Kentucky Horse Park;
Lexington, Kentucky.

Roughhewn Grace: The Blount Mansion (1798).
Knoxville, Tennessee.

The City-County Building, the First Baptist Church, and the University of Tennessee.
Knoxville, Tennessee.

155

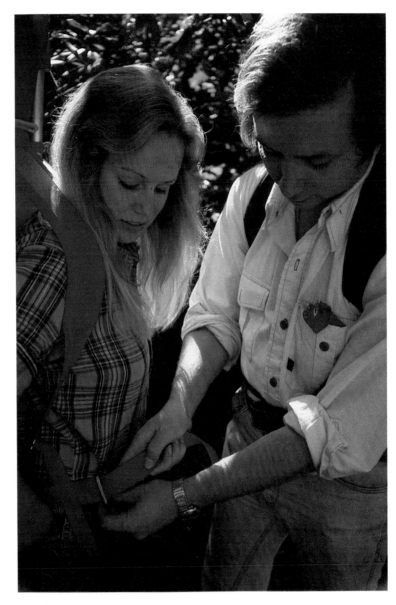

David and Lisa.
Great Smoky Mountains National Park, Tennessee.

Appalachian Intermezzo.
Smooth Shoulder Ridge, Tennessee.

The Volunteer Life and Dome Buildings, and Old Stone Church Tower.
Chattanooga, Tennessee.

Chattanooga and Lookout Mountain from the Walnut Street Bridge.
Chattanooga, Tennessee.

159

Lunch Hour at Miller Park.
Chattanooga, Tennessee.

The Sculpture Garden.
Hunter Museum of Art; Chattanooga, Tennessee.

McClellan Island: Dawn on the Tennessee River.
Chattanooga, Tennessee.

161

Downtown from Techwood Street.
Atlanta, Georgia.

The Omni.
Atlanta, Georgia.

High Shoals of the Apalachee.
Morgan County, Georgia.

Let's Keep Pulling Together, Atlanta.
Atlanta, Georgia.

163

Five Points and the Flatiron Building.
Atlanta, Georgia.

The Varsity: Drive-In to Generations.
Atlanta, Georgia.

Hot Dogs, Hamburgers, and ''Little House on the Prairie.''
The Varsity; Atlanta, Georgia.

The Confrontation: Rapid Transit Construction at the Northeast Expressway.
Atlanta, Georgia.

Education from Another Era.
The Old Central School; Oconee County, Georgia.

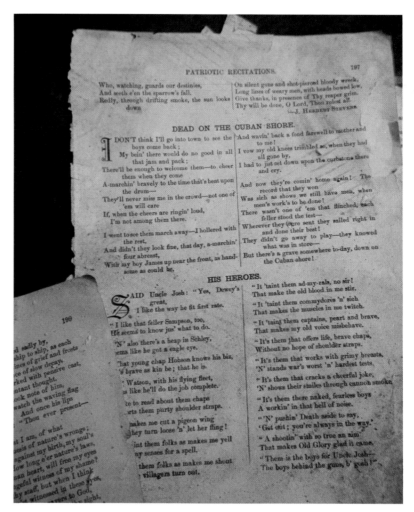

Patriotic Recitations.
Spanish-American War Reader. The Old Central School.

Country Pride.
Oconee County, Georgia.

Six-Score Autumns.
Fort Payne, Alabama.

Georgia Backroads.
Walnut Creek; Hall County.

Durham's Alcove.
Fort Payne, Alabama.

Birmingham from Red Mountain.
Alabama.

Liberty-in-Miniature.
Woodrow Wilson Park;
Birmingham, Alabama.

Serene Sunday.
East Lake Park; Birmingham, Alabama.

Overspreading Oaks.
Madison Avenue; Montgomery, Alabama.

McMonnies Fountain.
Court Square; Montgomery, Alabama.

173

On Duty.
Mobile, Alabama.

The Alabama State Capitol.
Montgomery.

174

Moving Upriver at Dawn.
Mobile, Alabama.

175

Relaxed Mood.
Bellingrath Gardens; Mobile, Alabama.

Trawler Southern Breeze; Tow Crimson Tide.
Mobile, Alabama.

The Valley Cafe.
Kingston, Arkansas.

Hybrid Beauties.
Bellingrath Gardens; Mobile, Alabama.

Women's Rally.
Little Rock, Arkansas.

Capitol Avenue.
Little Rock, Arkansas.

Children at Play.
War Memorial Park; Little Rock, Arkansas.

180

Bluffs on the Buffalo.
Steel Creek Access Area;
Buffalo National River,
Arkansas.

Dallas is to New York, as Fort Worth is to Chicago, as Kansas City is to St. Louis

We were talking earlier about sister cities that can be so much alike in some ways and so very different in others. Some sister cities you come across are barely even step-sisters; they're not alike in *any* way. Minneapolis and St. Paul are that way. So are Oakland and San Francisco. And to get to the point, Dallas and Fort Worth may be only a long taxi ride apart, but they've always struck me as wholly different.

Dallas is the sophisticated sun-tanned long-legged sister that grew up beautiful and married rich and drove a Lincoln Continental half as long as the road to Waxahachie. Fort Worth is the red-headed gal who grew up in freckles and hand-me-down jeans. She drives a stick-shift Mustang with the kids holding on in the rumble seat. She looks you straight in the eye and she shakes hands hard. None of this business of kiss on the cheek. I will give you a long equation: Dallas is to New York, as Fort Worth is to Chicago, as Kansas City is to St. Louis, as Tulsa is to Oklahoma City. Factor these out, and you come up with answers in imaginary numbers. Some sisters drink tea and some drink coffee; some chew gum and some don't. They all have distinctive personalities, but they're *different* personalities.

None of this is to suggest that Fort Worth is little more than an overgrown cowtown. The city boasts an opera company, a first-rate symphony, three excellent museums of art. Architect Philip Johnson's Water Garden is a thing of beauty. On formal occasions in Fort Worth, men get into black ties and dinner jackets just as they do anywhere else. It's just that collars are more likely to be buttoned down in Dallas and Houston, and left open in Fort Worth. Cowboy boots seem a little affected in Dallas; they don't hurt anyone's feet in Fort Worth.

The city had its beginning in 1849, when Major General William J. Worth ordered a string of eight forts built across the state. His engineers named the first one after him. The line was to mark the frontier. To the east was the U.S.A.—white man's country. To the west was Indian country. From that day to this, as any friend of Amon Carter could have told you, Dallas is where the East peters out and Fort Worth is where the West begins.

It's hard to think of Fort Worth without thinking of Amon Carter. Some men and some families personify cities—Jimmy Walker and Fiorello LaGuardia in New York, Henry W. Grady in Atlanta, Boss Crump in Memphis, the Bryans in Richmond, the Daniels in Raleigh, the Binghams in Louisville. To a remarkable degree, Amon was the romping, stomping, hat-waving, gut-busting high-living embodiment of Fort Worth. He started out a poor boy, selling turkey drumsticks and chicken sandwiches through the windows of the trains that came by Bowie, Texas. He scrabbled and he struggled; he was a teen-aged wheeler-dealer, and after a while he wound up selling advertising in Fort Worth. This was just after the turn of the century.

Amon could sell anything. In the end he was selling only two products: He was selling Fort Worth and Amon G. Carter, but now he was selling newspaper ads for the fledgling Fort Worth *Star*. It was a sick chick of a newspaper, but when he had a chance to buy a piece of it he borrowed $250 and tried to run up his stake in a poker game. Characteristically, he lost most of his wad to a queen-high straight against his own three aces. He held on, fighting every inch of the way, and though the paper almost died Carter survived. Eventually he merged the falling *Star* with the profitable *Telegram,* and by 1912 he had a nice little monopoly going.

He made the most of it. He made millions and he spent millions, and in the early thirties he went into wildcatting and he lost millions. He was down to pawning his diamond rings when one of his rigs lucked into the Wasson pool in West Texas. He never was poor after that. He used to give away favors that ranged down from hundred-dollar Stetson hats. You knew how you stood with Amon by what he gave you for Christmas. You could move up in his esteem from grapefruit to turkeys to pecans to whiskey-canes to those legendary hats. Or you could move down.

Carter could be the most generous man in Texas, which is saying a whole lot, but he could be a mean-tempered sumbitch when the mood was on him. He was like the nobleman that Sam Johnson once described: Lord Bathurst "hated a fool, and he hated a rogue, and he hated a whig; he was a very good hater." Carter hated frauds, he hated Baptist preachers, he hated Lyndon Johnson, naturally he hated Dallas. Invited to a fancy luncheon club in Dallas, he once brought his own sandwich in a paper sack.

Sometimes he got over his mads, sometimes he cherished them for years. Back in 1935 he got mad at Dallas—unusually mad at Dallas—and began looking for a way to get even. He dreamed up an exposition that would put Dallas at the penny-ante table. Skeptics said he'd never pull it off. It couldn't be done. Carter did it. He hired showman Billy Rose at a thousand dollars a day to supervise the venture, and Billy Rose hired Sally Rand to run a Nude Ranch. On the opening day of the Fort Worth Frontier Centennial, July 18, 1936, Amon Carter drove a Wells Fargo stage-coach into the grounds. He was dressed, as he so often was, in full cowboy regalia with six-guns slung from his hips. He let 'em rip.

Amon had invited a thousand correspondents and columnists to attend the opening. He gave them good beef barbecue and all the high-class post-Prohibition booze they could manage, and they wrote their heads off. Before the show closed in November, more than two million persons visited the exposition and gawked at the Billy Rose girls. It was an artistic success but a financial disaster. Rose had gone through his budget like a strip-dancer through her first petticoat. The investors lost their stakes but Fort Worth prospered and Dallas fumed. Amon was the happiest man in Texas.

In the years that followed the exposition, Carter hobnobbed with presidents and senators and governors. The *Star-Telegram* covered West Texas like a range of mes-quite. Nothing of importance happened in Abilene, Big Spring, Midland or Odessa that failed to make the early edition. Carter decreed weather reporting never seen before or since. He chronicled rainfall in Barnhart, Lobo, Tarzan and Wink—towns practically nobody ever heard of. Until an illness felled him in 1953, he seemed the inexhaustible man. He died two years later at 75, and some of the spirit of West Texas went with him—hat, boots, six-guns and all.

Houston has some of the hand-tooled, hundred-buck ebullience of Fort Worth, and Houston has known its fabulous characters also—Will Hogg, Jesse Jones, Oveta Hobby—but Houston's personality is different. The city has grown like a teen-aged boy; its pants never seem exactly to fit. In the thirty years between 1950 and 1980, Houston added a million residents; more than two-thirds of its people have no more roots than a tumbleweed. The city's skyline might have been created by a blind man throwing skyscrapers at a dartboard—here a cluster, there a cluster.

Everything about Houston is Texas-sized. George Fuermann wrote a book about the city. He tells of the Houston woman who reported to police that her mink stole had been stolen. Where had it been stolen? From her pickup truck. In front of a new

The Atrium.
Plaza of the Americas; Dallas, Texas.

Simple Gifts.
Trinity River Greenbelt; Dallas, Texas.

187

apartment house, a sign appeals to rising executives: "Your Subordinates Cannot Afford to Live Here." Houston has an airport so far out of town that some passengers just walk over from San Antonio. Local sports fans decided it was too danged hot to watch baseball out-of-doors, so they built an air-conditioned pleasure dome beyond the dreams of Kubla Khan.

San Antonio is more in scale with its surroundings. It too has grown, but at a gentler pace, melding the diverse cultures of Spanish, Anglos and Germans. Like Baltimore, the city has tackled its urban problems with imagination. The riverway, once a desolate sewer, has been transformed into an area of surpassing charm. An old brewery now houses a fine arts museum. San Antonio's Spanish-speaking population is half again as large as Miami's, but this 260-year-old Texas city seems to have avoided factitious animosities. San Antonio is warm; it is friendly; it is awakening to human and geographical resources that were there all along.

It's a long haul from San Antonio to El Paso, but El Paso is another city with a rich hispanic heritage, and I recommend it to you. Travelers in Texas shouldn't miss Austin, if only for the LBJ Library there. I was born in Oklahoma City—a small town in 1920—and I never cease to marvel at how the old place has grown . . . and grown . . . and grown. There used to be quite a rivalry between Oklahoma City and Tulsa. The Tulsans tended to regard us as social inferiors, and maybe this was true. Tulsa had the culture and we had the oil wells. You pays your money and you takes your choice. These days Tulsa is as pleasant a city as you will find in the whole country, notable among other things for Oral Roberts University. More things have been wrought by radio prayers than Tulsa's town fathers ever dreamed of.

High Plains Crossroad.
Inadale, Texas.

Refuge in the City.
Thanks·Giving Square; Dallas, Texas.

Eloquence at Dusk: Reunion Park and the Hyatt Regency Hotel.
Dallas, Texas.

The Inter-American Arrives at Union Station.
Dallas, Texas.

1880s Bandstand.
Old City Park; Dallas, Texas.

"Pegasus and Man" (Carl Milles, 1949).
Cullen/Frost Bank; Dallas, Texas.

191

B. B. King at Billy Bob's Texas.
Fort Worth.

West Seventh Avenue.
Fort Worth, Texas.

193

"The Eagle" (Alexander Calder, 1974).
Fort Worth National Bank;
Fort Worth, Texas.

The Home Place—Texas Style.
River Oaks; Houston, Texas.

The Wortham Fountains.
Tranquility Park; Houston, Texas.

Galleria I.
Houston, Texas.

Form Follows Function.
Sam Houston Park; Houston, Texas.

Freeway Interchange.
The Gulf Freeway and
the Southwest Freeway; Houston, Texas.

Texas Posh: River Oaks Country Club.
Houston, Texas.

198

Spring Air.
West 17th and South Harrison;
Amarillo, Texas.

The Lamb Sale.
South Plains Fairgrounds; Lubbock, Texas.

The Lee & Mary E. Bivins Home (detail).
Amarillo, Texas.

Judge Roy Bean's Trading Post.
Amarillo, Texas.

San Jacinto Plaza.
El Paso, Texas.

Where Regions Meet.
El Paso, Texas.

203

Congress Avenue and the Capitol.
Austin, Texas.

Spring Showers at Main Plaza.
San Antonio, Texas.

Rosndio Sanchez.
Chisos Remuda; Big Bend National Park, Texas.

Workers at the Littlefield Home.
University of Texas at Austin.

Kitch at the Capitol.
Austin, Texas.

Waterfront and Ship Channel.
Galveston, Texas.

Mural and Museum Store.
The Museum of Texas Tech University; Lubbock, Texas.

Saturday Night at the Texas.
Sweetwater, Texas.

Reflections at the Sheraton.
Corpus Christi, Texas.

Robert S. Kerr Park.
Oklahoma City, Oklahoma.

1889.
The Land Rush Memorial;
Oklahoma City, Oklahoma.

The Plaza.
Oklahoma City, Oklahoma.

Plains Wheat.
Custer City, Oklahoma.

Lunch-Hour Entertainment.
Dewey F. Bartlett Square; Tulsa, Oklahoma.

Skyscrapers Will Dwarf Silos.
S. Boston Street; Tulsa, Oklahoma.

The Power of Prayer.
The City of Faith; Tulsa, Oklahoma.

Thus ends this meandering odyssey. I go back to the point of beginning. By every statistical index, the old rural South of the Nashville Agrarians has melded into a predominantly urban region. That trend surely will continue. Skyscrapers will dwarf silos, and we scarcely will hear the tractors for the rush of jet planes. And yet—and yet. No matter how many Southerners move to city streets, an umbilical tie to the old ways will never be wholly severed. From the lofty windows of the Petroleum Club in Houston or the Summit Club in Columbia, we look beyond the streetlights of good cities to the enduring resources of a good land.

Reflections in the City of Faith (under construction, 1981).
Tulsa, Oklahoma.

209

Designed by Robert L. Nance

Text composed in Linotron Palatino by
Akra Data, Inc., Birmingham, Alabama

Color Separations by
Capitol Engraving Company, Nashville, Tennessee

Text Paper is Vintage Gloss by
Northwest Paper Division, Potlatch Corporation, Cloquet, Minnesota

Endleaves are Antique Rainbow by
Ecological Fibers, Inc., Lancaster, Massachusetts

Cover Cloth is Record Buckram by
The Holliston Mills, Inc., Kingsport, Tennessee

Printed and bound by
Kingsport Press, Inc., Kingsport, Tennessee